The
Rescue Dog

hamlyn

THE Rescue Dog

Gwen Bailey

Foreword by
Katie Boyle

'For Beau — who helped me realise how much could be achieved.'

Author's note

I have referred to 'he' rather than 'she' throughout
this book. There is no reason for this other than to save
writing he/she or it each time. There is no difference
between the worth of male and female dogs —
both have qualities that can make them rewarding,
lifelong companions.

Executive Editor: Julian Brown
Project Editor: Tarda Davison-Aitkins
Design: Les Needham
Picture Research: Zoe Holtermann
Production Controller: Sarah Scanlon

First published in Great Britain in 2000
by Hamlyn, an imprint of
Octopus Publishing Group Limited
2–4 Heron Quays, London, E14 4JP

Copyright © 2000 Octopus Publishing Group Limited

This paperback edition first published by Hamlyn in 2001

0 600 60351 2

A catalogue record for this book is available from the British Library

Produced by Toppan
Printed in China

Contents

*Katie Boyle and her
Battersea Belles.*

Foreword

Rescue dogs of all sorts, sizes and ages have always been an integral part of my own life. The only thing they had in common was that they'd all been abandoned or were victims of cruelty. This left them with loads of hang-ups, both mental and physical.

A long time ago in my native Italy, I was taught that being gentle and kind to them would, somehow, be sufficient. That loving them would make them understand us and would make them want to please us and do as they were told. This well-meaning, but amateurish attitude to dogs in need was a good start, but not enough. I learned later of the 'Think Dog' approach and how best to communicate with them. The methods and information in this book take us further and teach us what else we need to do to ensure a perfect partnership.

I've watched Gwen Bailey's rehabilitating methods in action. Her gentle, calm approach and sixth sense of understanding towards her two- and four-legged pupils are so reassuring to both dogs and people alike, and remarkably effective.

Sadly, there are still, and always will be, far too many homeless dogs to fill the number of homes available, and, every day, hundreds of healthy young animals are put to sleep. Luckily, there is also an increasing number of people who would like to give a good and happy home to an adult dog, but who are apprehensive of the problems that are likely to crop up. For them, this book will be reassuring and a much needed 'bible' to turn to for direction. I shall keep it as my permanent bedside reading too.

I am so glad what Gwen has filled a much-needed gap for dog lovers. This book is a treasure chest of information and guidance.

KATIE BOYLE

Introduction

Taking on an adult dog can be an exciting and rewarding experience that saves a dog's life and provides a family with a much loved friend. Making sure you are well prepared before taking a new pet into your home is the object of this book. It aims to give you the information you need to choose the right dog for you and your family and to make it easy to start off your relationship on the right foot. It will also provide ideas for teaching your new dog how you want him to behave, aid understanding and communication and will ease you through the early stages when you will both be adjusting to living together.

It is a sad fact that many dogs that are acquired with such high expectations as puppies do not stay with one set of owners for life. For the past 10 years, I have worked as the Animal Behaviourist for The Blue Cross, one of Britain's largest animal welfare charities. I have helped to sort out problems which have arisen between a new dog and its owner, given advice to new owners to help dogs settle in more easily and provide a back-up advice for when anything goes wrong. This book is an attempt to reach people who would otherwise not benefit from this service. Dogs and new owners are so varied that a book cannot possibly contain all you need to know, but it can give you some important guidelines to start you off on the right foot and help you avoid basic mistakes that can so easily result in the dog being returned. It will help you to select and keep a companion that will, hopefully, spend many happy years as an important member of your family.

Authors acknowledgements

I would like to thank John Rogerson, a talented and resourceful friend, who taught me so much about dog behaviour. The quality of the information he gave was such that I have been able to introduce behavioural concepts to help with rescue and rehoming at The Blue Cross and at other shelters throughout the world. Without his generosity in sharing his knowledge none of this would have been possible. I would also like to thank others who have shared their ideas and information so willingly with me over the years. They include Ian Dunbar, Tony Orchard, Peter Neville and the late John Fisher.

Several friends read the manuscript. They are Paul Barney, Katie Boyle, Andrew Edney, Elaine Grainger, Tony Orchard, Julie Sellors, Patches Silverstone and my parents. Thank you to you all for your help, encouragement and friendship.

As my employer for the past decade, The Blue Cross also deserves my thanks for allowing me to develop ways of introducing behaviour work to the rescue world. This has allowed me to help more dogs and owners than I would have thought possible and has given us new techniques and experience to pass on to others working in the field.

Publishers acknowledgements

Hamlyn would like to thank the The Blue Cross and the following people for giving up their time, lending their dogs and modelling in this book; Sally Reed; Charlotte Potts; Ginny Mabbort; Josh Perry; Linda Dixon; Tina Kew; Selina Williams; Alex Gilmore; Jo Heatherington; Lin Rogers; Georgina Parker (all from The Blue Cross); Adam Ward; Peter Burt; Mr & Mrs May; D. Millard; Carl & Louise Cross; John Stone; Kay Kentfield; Ian Shields; Diane Ward; Diane Blackburn; Samantha Visick; Andrea Fraser; T. Millard & Family; Sharon Lum; Sarah Allcock; Helen Murray; Dinah Wilkins and Katrina Moore.

The Blue Cross is one of Britain's leading animal welfare charities, providing advice, practical care, veterinary treatment and rehoming for thousands of companion animals each year.

CHAPTER

1

Which is the Right Dog for You?

A rescue dog can be a delight or a disaster. Which it is depends largely on choosing the right dog to suit your personality and that of your family. Every owner or family is different and will have different requirements. Fortunately, rescue dogs come in a wide variety of shapes, sizes and temperaments. All you have to do is put some time and thought into finding one that will be exactly right for you.

Rescue dogs come in many different shapes, sizes and temperaments.

New owners will often base their choice of dog on appearance only. They will often be persuaded by a dog that most closely resembles one they had as a child or previously owned. It is not wise to choose a dog in this way as no consideration is given to the temperament of that particular dog. A dog that attracts you instantly may bite your children or fight with your other dog, whereas a dog that has been chosen to have the right mixture of characteristics and temperament traits is much more likely to settle in easily and become a perfect pet. Having said that, appearances do count and it is also important that you are able to fall in love with the dog that you choose.

Deciding what you want

If you decide to skip this part, be warned that you may end up with a rescued dog that is less than perfect for you. A dog with traits that do not suit you, such as one with too much energy for

Small dogs are often in short supply at rescue centres as they are more popular than larger dogs.

your lifestyle, or one which is constantly harassing your cat/rabbit/child, can be awful to live with. Such dogs may make a perfectly nice pet for someone else, but you will have the wrong dog for you. Careful thought at this stage can help you to avoid the common trap of falling for the first pretty face you see. So often this results in a frustrated dog and a disappointed owner. It's a bit like finding a husband/wife/partner really!

Before you even go near an animal shelter, you need to sit down with all the people who will be involved with the new dog on a regular basis and find out what sort of dog you are looking for. There are some fundamental questions that will need answers before you can begin your search. These fall into two categories – physical attributes and temperament traits.

PHYSICAL ATTRIBUTES

You will probably find it easier to decide which physical attributes would suit you rather than what type of temperament you are looking for, but both are equally important.

Size

The size of your home and garden will limit the size of dog that it is practical for you to keep. A large dog in a small flat is not sensible and a little one that can curl up in the corner of the sofa may be more suitable. Size is often less important than how active a dog likes to be – see page 16. However, be realistic about the size of dog that may suit your home and lifestyle. Even if you have always wanted to own a Newfoundland or a Bernese Mountain Dog, you may not have the facilities to keep one properly.

Consider also what you want a dog for. If your lifestyle dictates that you often need to take your dog on a train and bus, a little dog you can tuck under your arm may be more appropriate. If you live in an area where it's dangerous to walk the streets, you may want a dog that at least looks as though it will protect you.

If you already have a dog, it is important to get one of a similar size for when they play together or fight. Boisterous play between dogs of unequal size can result in substantial injuries to

FACTORS TO CONSIDER

Before you choose your dog, you must decide which physical attributes and which temperament traits are important to you. Use the following check list to remind you what you need to consider.

Physical attributes:
- Size
- Male or female
- Neutered or not
- Age
- Type of coat

Temperament traits:
- Which breed?
- Good with children
- Good with other pets
- Good with strangers
- Good with other dogs
- Energy levels
- How strong-willed?
- How cuddly?
- How trainable?
- How independent?

the smaller dog. Similarly, if they do fight during the settling in period, the damage to the smaller animal can be potentially fatal if there is a large difference in size.

Male or female?

There is more chance of finding a dog to suit you if you decide you want a male. There are slightly more males than females in rescue centres and many potential owners tend to prefer females because they assume that bitches will be better behaved and more biddable. While it is true that male dogs are more likely to get into trouble and behave badly at some time in their lives, particularly during adolescence, female dogs also cause their fair share of troubles.

Dogs that have suffered physical or mental abuse are sometimes looking for a home. They can make wonderful pets.

Approximately six males to every four females are seen by pet behaviour counsellors. Male dogs tend to be slightly more aggressive and competitive from an early age, which can lead to difficulties if not channelled in the right direction. However, a good-natured male dog may make a much better pet than a bad-tempered female and, as the character of an adult dog is already formed, it is wise to leave your options open rather than limit yourself because of the misconception that one sex will be better than the other.

The only time when it is worth paying particular attention to whether a dog is male or female is if you already have a dog. Dogs of the opposite sex living together in a household are usually far more likely to get along than two of the same sex and will have fewer arguments. But again this depends on the individual's character (see page 15 for more information on choosing a dog to live with an existing dog).

Neutered or entire?

Many of the bigger rescue organisations neuter all their animals as a matter of course. Usually this is because they see, at first hand, the tragedy of too many pets for too few good homes. Neutering ensures that reproduction stops with the pets that go through their hands.

Generally, neutered animals have the advantage. Neutered male dogs are less likely to get into

Young or old? Age is often one of the easiest criteria to decide on.

trouble with other males, less likely to mount soft furnishings or people, and less likely to get out and roam or be frustrated if there is a bitch in season nearby. Neutered females do not have the nuisance of seasons every six months. And all neutered animals are less likely to develop hormone-related problems later in life.

Age

More younger dogs, usually those between one and two years' old, are given up to rescue centres than older dogs. The younger a dog is, the more active it is likely to be as, like humans, dogs tend to slow down as they get older. A young dog is also more likely to have less than perfect behaviour because people often acquire puppies that they neglect and give up to a rescue home or turn out when the cute puppy stage has worn off.

While a younger dog will be less set in its ways and will adapt itself more readily to a new lifestyle, dogs of all ages are very adaptable and most will fit in eventually. You can teach an old dog new tricks, but it may take slightly longer than teaching the same tricks to a younger one. Older dogs will live for fewer years, which may be an advantage if you are elderly yourself. They will be more likely to tolerate being left at home while you go to work and they will hopefully have a track record of living successfully as a pet dog. Difficult dogs are more likely to have to be euthanased at an early age.

'You __can__ teach an old dog new tricks ... '

Coat type

Coat types can be roughly divided into short (labrador), medium (collie or spaniel), long or thick (samoyed or bearded collie), or the type that needs to be clipped regularly (poodle). Special care is needed for long or thick hair or hair that needs to be clipped and you need to decide if you want that level of responsibility.

Short coats shed hairs that may weave themselves into your clothes in a way that you never thought possible and medium length coats seem to bring back most of the mud you encounter on a walk. There are advantages and disadvantages to every type; be prepared for extra mess with whatever type of coat you choose.

TEMPERAMENT TRAITS

A dog's temperament is more important than how it looks.

Breed

The original dog breeds were developed for different jobs in the service of man and have different characteristics and abilities as a result. If you have your heart set on a pedigree dog, read about its temperament traits in the various breed books available, but do read between the lines. Such books will rarely tell you the pitfalls of the breed, but you can often work these out for yourself. Remember that every positive trait has a down side to it if it is not correctly channelled or it does not suit your household. For example, for 'lively' read 'can be exhausting', for 'determined and strong-willed' read 'can be stubborn and domineering', for 'good guard dog' read 'can be aggressive'. Ask people who already own one of your chosen breed about the good and bad traits in their dogs.

Dogs bred for working purposes, such as sheep dogs, gundogs or some hounds, often have natural energy levels that enable them to keep active all day. In an average home, this amount of energy is often too much and an owner will need to be inventive in finding outlets for it. Conversely, dogs bred for the show ring have often inherited genes that makes them lazier, but not always. Crossbreeds and

Crosses of breeds like collies usually inherit a strong desire to chase, play and be very active.

GENETIC TRAITS AND TENDENCIES

This is a general guide based on a cross-section of dogs of these breeds or crosses. It will, however, be possible to find dogs from these categories who do not fit this description.

BORDER COLLIE
Very active; prone to fears, noise phobias and nipping when scared; forms very strong bonds with owner; loyal; likes to chase; playful; needs lots of exercise and stimulation; often needs experienced owners.

COLLIE CROSS
Very reactive; prone to shyness; noise sensitive; can nip when severely frightened; easily scared; sensitive; forms very strong, rewarding bond with owner; loyal; playful; likes to chase; active and energetic.

DOBERMANN
Sensitive; can be strong willed; can be boisterous and clumsy; forms strong bond with owners.

GERMAN SHEPHERD CROSS
Likely to be good guard dog, but prone to territorial aggression, especially if shy or fearful; forms strong, rewarding bond with owner; loyal; sensitive; very loving to family; likes to chase; often quite vocal.

LURCHER/GREYHOUND
Friendly; independent and tends not to over-bond to owners; likes to run and hunt on a walk, but usually calm around the house; inclined to show predatory behaviour to smaller animals.

LABRADOR CROSS
Less reactive than collie crosses; generally good natured and tolerant; playful; can be boisterous; inclined to chew when young; can be good for a lively household.

SPANIEL
Usually very biddable; playful and willing to please; often have gentle, loving nature; good family dog if raised correctly; can be possessive of food and toys; needs lots of exercise.

STAFFORDSHIRE BULL TERRIER
Can be problematic with other dogs, but often very nice with humans; can be quite vocal; physically insensitive and may pull on lead; can be a good family dog and enjoy games with toys; can show sustained aggression if upset.

TERRIER CROSS
Lively; curious; independent; full of character; can show sustained aggression if upset; can be strong-willed.

If you have children, finding a dog that is used to them and enjoys their company is essential.

mongrels will have inherited a combination of genes and the advantage of taking on such an adult dog is that its genes have already fulfilled their potential and you can see exactly what you are getting.

Good with children

You will need to decide how important it is that your new dog will be friendly and unafraid of children. This is obviously one of the most important considerations if you have children or grandchildren, or if other children visit you on a regular basis.

Bear in mind that children vary enormously and a dog that has been brought up with older children may not be able to tolerate toddlers that fall on him, pinch him or pull his ears. Teenagers, who are often going through difficult times, may have once been intentionally cruel to a dog, which may then be very wary of people of similar ages. Or the dog who fits all your other requirements may have been teased by school-age children of which you have three at home.

Different dogs will have different tolerance levels to things that children are likely to do them. If you have loud, boisterous children, you will need a dog that can tolerate this. If you have quiet, gentle children, your dog will not need to be so tolerant. Make a family decision about what age groups your dog will need to be friendly with and tolerant of.

Good with other pets

If you have a cat or a smaller pet, such as a rabbit or bird, you will need to select a dog that does not want to chase, catch and eat it. Cats, especially, can suffer from the unwanted attentions of a new dog and may take to living outside because it is too unsafe to live inside. Selecting a dog that will quickly settle in with a cat is not easy, but it should be a major consideration if you have one.

Good with strangers

Consider how many visitors you have and how many strangers you and your family meet and interact with on a regular basis. This will tell you how important it is for your new dog to be unafraid and sociable with strangers.

    If you live a quiet life in a fairly isolated area, it will not matter if your dog is unsociable; in fact it may be advantageous since you will probably benefit from its desire to protect you and your territory from unwanted attention. However, if you run a business from home or you live in a busy household with plenty of visitors, if you like to stop and chat to other dog walkers and enjoy taking your dog everywhere with you, you will need one that is friendly and happy in the company of everyone.

A dog that barks at strangers will suit some families but not others.

Good with other dogs

There are two issues to consider when talking about other dogs: how important is it that your new dog gets on with another dog in the family or one that you have regular contact with? And how important is it that he gets on with other dogs when out on walks?

How sociable your new dog is with other dogs will determine how easily he can be taken for walks.

Most dogs will get used to and tolerate another dog that they have regular dealings with, particularly if they are introduced properly. However, being sociable with other dogs you meet outside requires your dog to have more social skills. Living with a dog that is afraid, anxious or aggressive in the company of other dogs may not be too difficult if you plan to take all your exercise in the country, but it could be very tedious if you live in a built-up area and intend to walk in a busy park.

Energy levels

Living with a dog that is always raring to go and that gets up expectantly whenever you make a move is fine if you are the active sort who enjoys plenty of activity and long walks. If you are not, however, it may be simpler to find a dog whose idea of heaven is a warm bed with the occasional wander up the street and back. Matching your new dog's activity level to your own will prevent your new dog becoming frustrated and a nuisance because it is under-exercised and will save you from traipsing the countryside when you would rather be tucked up in a chair with a good book. Getting this right is essential to stress-free ownership.

Owning a dog that likes to run and play is ideal if you have a lifestyle to match.

You will also need to match your desire to play games with your new dog to his desire to play with you. Some dogs are very playful and will constantly present you with a toy or other items in an attempt to encourage you to play. If this is not something you will enjoy, try to find a dog that is not so interested in games.

Dogs that have plenty of mental and physical energy can find it difficult to lie down all day and sleep while their owners are at work. If you have to leave your dog at home for long periods, it is sensible to look for a dog that enjoys sleeping a lot rather than getting an active dog or youngster who will become bored and cause problems when left alone.

How strong-willed?

Pushy dogs fare much better with strong-willed owners and gentle dogs are happier with sensitive people. You need to consider how insistent you will be that your dog will conform to your rules. If you or other members of your family will be insistent and can be a bit overbearing at times, choose a dog that has a strong character as you may overpower a weaker character. Dogs with stronger characters usually have more spirit, are more confident and independent, and often learn faster.

If, however, you are a gentle owner who is very tolerant and indulgent, find a dog that is sensitive and submissive. If you choose a stronger character, he may choose to take control once he has had the opportunity to assess your abilities. Choosing a gentle dog if you are a sensitive owner will often result in a trusting and close bond that is beneficial to both parties. Dogs with gentle characters are often more tolerant of children and other animals and are often less confident of their ability to use aggression in a difficult situation.

How cuddly?

Dogs do not naturally hold and hug each other unless they are fighting or mating, whereas humans cuddle each other and other animals as an expression of love and affection. Dogs need to learn that humans do this and learn to tolerate and enjoy it. Some dogs enjoy being touched and cuddled more than others. If you are someone who likes to stroke and hug your dog a lot, find one that enjoys it or you may be disappointed when he starts to avoid you when you reach out to him.

How trainable?

All dogs can be trained once you know how, but some learn faster than others. Some dogs will know a few commands already, but the majority know only the word 'sit'. If you want a really well trained dog, it is best to

'If, however, you are a gentle owner who is very tolerant and indulgent, find a dog that is sensitive and submissive. If you choose a stronger character, he may choose to take control once he has had the opportunity to assess your abilities.'

find one that is very trainable (see page 32) and acquire the skills needed to train him yourself.

How independent?

Many dogs do not enjoy being separated from their owners. All dogs will have to put up with it once in a while, but if you plan to leave your dog on a regular basis, such as while you are at work, look for a dog that is happy to be left alone. Dogs that are destructive, noisy or dirty when left alone are usually not happy and it would not be wise to take on a dog that does this if you cannot be with it for most of the time.

Finding a dog that does not mind being left alone is essential if you plan to be away from home frequently.

OTHER CHARACTERISTICS TO CONSIDER

There will be other characteristics not listed above that will be special to you and your family. Consider what an average day for your dog will be like and list all the characteristics that would enable your dog to cope easily with it. If you plan to take your dog to work every day, for example, it should enjoy travelling. Problems relating to car travel can be overcome (see page 144), but if your dog will be travelling often, it may be easier and more sensible to choose a dog that enjoys car travel.

Where to find rescue dogs

Once you have your agreed list of physical attributes and temperament traits, the next step is to choose a source of dogs available for adoption. There are many places where unwanted dogs can be found. The major sources are animal centres run by large national charities such as The Blue Cross, large dogs' homes in cities, breed rescue organisations, from friends or through an advertisement, although the latter is not recommended.

Opposite bottom: Staff at a good rescue centre will be able to give you accurate information and help you make your choice.

When you do go to see a particular dog, ensure that the whole family and anyone who will have regular dealings with your dog goes with you. It is essential that everyone likes the dog and gets on with it as much as you do.

RESCUE CENTRES AND DOGS' HOMES

There are many large rescue organisations that have centres around the country such as The Blue Cross, the National Canine Defence League, the RSPCA and the SSPCA. There is also a variety of smaller, independent charities and there is usually a large dogs' home in most major cities, such as The Dogs' Home, Battersea. The larger dogs' homes often have as many animals as the larger rescue organisations keep throughout the entire country. This gives you more choice, but it means that less information is likely to be available about each individual due to the number of dogs that pass through.

There may be more than one centre or home in your area. To find out which one is best, ask other owners of rehomed dogs about their experiences, canvas your local dog training club (which will see many of the 'problem' rescued dogs) and ask your veterinary practice for their recommendation. Excellent facilities are not as important as good management. If centre staff socialise and play with the dogs every day, the dogs will be better adjusted and will fit into your life more

TIP

Always take all of your family with you when you visit a rescue centre to look for a new pet.

Bad behaviour is more likely to be seen at centres where staff do not have the time or inclination to socialise and play with the dogs in their care.

easily. Staff will also get to know them better and will be able to help you choose the right one for you, and you will be more likely to see the true nature of a dog rather than an institutionalised version.

The advantages of obtaining a dog from a reputable rescue centre are that you will be given as much information as possible about the dog you are taking on and your dog will be healthy and will have received a health check prior to leaving. It will probably also be vaccinated, neutered and insured. You should be offered useful advice to help you settle the dog in and an aftercare service if things begin to go wrong after rehoming. If things go dramatically wrong despite everyone's best intentions, the centre will be willing to take the dog back and find it a more suitable home.

An excellent service such as this is expensive for rescue organisations and it is only reasonable to give them a generous donation when you collect your new dog. Remember that they are only able to carry out their work because of donations: none of the UK rescue centres receives any state funding.

If you visit a small rescue centre, you may be unable to find a dog that is perfect for you on your first visit. Try not to be disheartened – the turnover in such establishments is usually quite quick and if you visit a few days later, there will probably be new dogs to see. The more friendly, easy-to-home dogs will go to new homes quite quickly so if you have very stringent requirements you will need to visit the centre often to ensure that your visits coincide with the arrival of new dogs.

BREED RESCUE ORGANISATIONS

If you are determined to own a particular breed of dog and would like to take on an adult rather than a puppy, the easiest route is to contact your nearest rescue organiser for the breed in question. The Kennel Club will be able to give you details of your nearest organisation

Breed rescue organisations vary tremendously in their quality. Some are very good, but some are very poor. They are usually run by a breeder who has many years' experience with a particular breed, but this does not necessarily mean they will be good at matching dogs to prospective owners. Ask around to find out what other's experiences have been; particularly ask your local rescue centre as they will usually have had some contact with each other. Your veterinary practice may also be a useful source of information.

THROUGH A FRIEND

This may be one of the best sources since you will know the dog and the owner. A good friend will not want to pass on a problem to you without letting you know first. However, it is unlikely that you will have a good friend who has to give up their dog at the very time that you happen to be looking for one. If you take on a dog because a friend has to give it up rather than because you are actively looking for one, think very carefully about whether you really do want it and consider beforehand all that dog ownership will entail.

VIA AN ADVERTISEMENT

This is probably the worst way to find the ideal dog for you. The 'Free to good home' ads are a potential minefield for new owners since you will have invested some emotion in the animal before you even see it. You will have read the description, been told about its good points over the phone and, by the time you get there, you will be thinking about where its bed will go and what colour collar to buy!

Unless there are very obvious flaws in a dog's character and behaviour, it will be very difficult to make an objective decision when you see it and you will have the added pressure from the owner who will want to pass the dog on. If they resort to any form of emotional blackmail, it will be difficult to resist, particularly if you have your family with you. My advice is to steer well clear of finding a rescue dog in this way unless you are very single-minded and resistant to your emotions.

Why are dogs rehomed?

People give up dogs for rehoming for all sorts of reasons. Often circumstances will dictate that they can no longer keep the dog. Owners die, are made redundant, lose their houses, get posted abroad, divorce and sometimes just cannot cope with life's pressures and a dog as well. Probably about 40 per cent of dogs go into the rescue system for these reasons rather than because there is anything wrong with their behaviour.

That leaves about 60 per cent of dogs that have been given up because their behaviour is less than perfect. A good proportion of these are not too badly behaved and will probably be perfectly all right if placed in a sensible, caring home. These dogs are usually the young ones whose owners have not put sufficient care and thought into their upbringing. They will need some

*Dogs that are problematic
in their first home may become
very well behaved in the next
if they are given more to do.*

work, but will make perfectly good pets.

A much smaller percentage of rescue dogs have a specific behaviour problem or problems that their owners were unable to cope with. Although an owner may be able to work round a problem during the first few years of a dog's life, when dramatic life changes occur, such as divorce or moving to a new area, the dog's problem may become too difficult to cope with. A dog that is perfectly behaved can usually fit into any lifestyle despite difficult circumstances, but a dog with problems is far more likely to be given up at times of emotional or physical upheaval. Such dogs will take their behaviour problems with them into their next home. These can be redeemed, but new owners will need to be aware of the problems so they can make an informed choice. They will also need to know how to reduce and eventually eliminate the problem.

STRAYS

Dogs found straying or abandoned, which are not claimed by their owners after seven days, are often put up for adoption. Unfortunately, nothing is known about these dogs. A small proportion are likely to be genuinely lost, but the majority will have belonged to owners who cared too little or who were too irresponsible to give them up to a rescue organisation. This tells you something about the previous owners of stray animals and it is, therefore, not surprising that there is often a slightly higher number of problem animals among strays than among dogs given up by their owners.

Despite this, strays should not be discounted altogether. Most can be placed in homes and will settle well, but they need more care to determine their characteristics.

Reliability of information

Good rescue organisations will take care to collect detailed information from previous owners to pass on to the next owner, but unfortunately not all owners tell the truth about their dogs. They may be too ashamed to admit they have raised a dog that has problems, they may not be able to see the problems at all or they may feel that the best chance for their dog lies in concealing anything they feel may reduce his chances of finding a home. Good rescue organisations will have experienced staff who are skilled at getting the truth and who are able to extract plenty of information.

The better rescue organisations will also have trained kennel staff who will be able to monitor a dog's behaviour and character while it lives at the kennels. This information can be invaluable in helping to match dogs to new owners. The dog's behaviour traits and problems often become apparent as a dog settles down to life in kennels and it will soon become obvious if the previous owner's testimony was correct or not.

The reliability of any information you receive about a dog will depend on the quality of staff at the centre and will vary considerably from centre to centre and even from person to person. Whether you decide to trust the information is up to you, but even if you do it is wise to have a back up in the form of the assessment procedures on pages 27 to 41. This will help you make your own notes about the dog to compare with the information you have been given. If there is a reasonable match, the chances are that the information from previous owners and kennel staff will have been offered and collected in good faith.

If you can, try to select from any written information a centre may provide a few dogs that look as though they may suit your needs. You will then be less likely to be persuaded by the dogs' appearances. If you have found a rescue centre where the staff are well trained and seem to know what they are talking about, take their advice on which dogs may suit you as they will know their dogs' characters better than you do. Take your time to talk to kennel staff and you may be surprised by how much information they are able to give to you.

Beware of the centre that offers very limited information or none at all. The dogs in these facilities will be no more or less worthy than in any others, but you will be on your own in terms of being able to determine which dog is right for you.

The adoption process

What actually happens at a rescue centre will depend on their procedures. Sometimes you will be shown particular dogs, sometimes you will be shown all the dogs, and sometimes you will be allowed to wander around on your own. You will probably be encouraged to take a potential pet out for a walk to get to know him or to take him into a special meeting room. Although staff will be busy, do ask for their help (see above/page xx). Tell them what type of dog you are looking for and ask for all the information they have on any dogs that suit your requirements. Armed with this information, you can set about assessing the dogs you think may make a suitable pet for you (see the assessment procedures given on pages 27 to 41).

When you have chosen a dog, you will need to reserve it. This will give you and the rescue centre staff time to decide whether this particular dog is right for you. Taking a dog home on the same day you find it is not a good idea as you do need time to make an objective decision. This can be difficult in the excitement generated by the occasion, but it becomes much easier after a few days of reflection. Sadly, this thinking time may not be possible at some of the larger dogs' homes where the pressure for kennel space is great. Try not to feel pressurised into making a decision. A new dog is likely to be with your family for the rest of its life and making a mistake at this stage can lead to much emotional turmoil.

Dogs that are able to spend time with each other and with people while in rescue centres will be more contented than those who are kept isolated.

A good rescue centre will ask you lots of questions about the type of dog you want, what your lifestyle and personality is like and why you want to adopt a dog. Be prepared to answer these questions patiently and honestly since it is in your own interest as well as that of the dog. Centre staff will also want to visit your home to check that you live where you say you do and that any fences around your property are secure. It also gives them a chance to give you more information about your dog and to answer any last minute questions.

A home visit will help to satisfy the staff that your home is just right and they will be able to answer any of your last minute questions.

CHAPTER

2

Finding your Perfect Rescue Dog

Having decided on the temperament traits and physical characteristics you are looking for, the search can now begin in earnest for a dog that matches the blueprint as closely as possible. It may be unrealistic to expect that you will find the perfect dog. If you look hard enough you may do so, but it is more likely that you will find a dog that almost fits your ideal. You can then assess whether or not you can live with the traits that are less than perfect and whether you can change his behaviour sufficiently for him to fit into your lifestyle.

Be realistic about what is achievable. It is not wise, for example, to take a shy dog that is afraid of strangers into a busy, lively and noisy household where it will be the centre of attention. A shy dog can be brought out of its shell with gentle understanding, but is unlikely to ever be the life and soul of a party.

Rescue centres can evoke a variety of emotions in even the most hardened people and it can be difficult to resist what seems to be rows of pitiful eyes and pleading faces. However, if it means you end up with a dog you can be happy with and that can be happy with you, it will be worth it. Do not be persuaded by the argument that unless you take a particular dog it will be put to sleep. It is wrong for rescue centres to use this type of emotional blackmail, however understandable it may be. You cannot save all the dogs in this predicament and you will not be doing the rescue world any favours if you take on a dog only to return it later because it does not fit into your lifestyle. Be single-minded about your search until you find a dog that meets your requirements as closely as possible.

Assessing a dog's character

Before making any assessment of a dog, ensure that he has been in kennels for at least three days. New dogs go through a settling in period during which time they behave in a depressed and unusual way. Only after they have adjusted to their new environment, which takes about three days, do they begin to behave as normal.

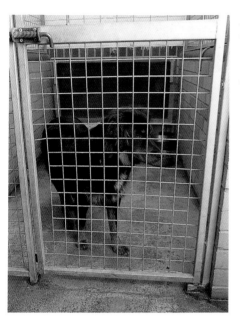

Dogs will not behave in kennels as thay would in a home. Information from staff and the results of your own tests will help you to make a realistic assessment of his character.

ASSESSMENT CHECKLIST

You will need to take the following items with you when you assess a dog:

- The whole family
- Titbits
- Toys (ball, tug-of-war toy, squeaky toy)
- Brush
- A small towel

Even after a dog has adjusted to life in kennels, he will not behave as he would in a pet home. Kennels can be hostile places no matter how well the dogs are looked after. This saps the confidence of even the most determined dog and there are fewer opportunities to misbehave. It is possible for a dog to appear perfectly behaved when you meet him in kennels and even when you take him out for a short time, but once he settles in to your home, he will revert to previous bad habits. You will not see the true picture so follow the assessment procedure below to find out more.

The assessment procedure

When you assess any dog, remember that you will see just a brief glimpse of a complex animal's character. While assessments are useful and necessary in helping you choose a dog that will be right for you, dogs do react to whatever is happening to them at the time. A dog may be tired, bored, hungry, lonely or frightened – all such emotions will affect his apparent behaviour. A dog will also behave differently towards you depending on whether you are male or female, and if you resemble someone he knew in his past this too can influence his behaviour.

Right: An initial interested reaction indicates that this dog will enjoy meeting visitors and your friends.

Far right: A fearful aggressive reaction shows that this dog mistrusts strangers and is likely to bark at visitors.

PART ONE

ASSESSMENT IN THE KENNEL

There is no scientific validation for the following assessment procedure at present, but it works for me and I think it is worth passing on. The initial part of the assessment is quick to do and can be done on any dog that looks as though he may have potential.

Approach each dog in exactly the same way and perform the same tests and you will be able to compare their responses. After numerous approaches to different dogs, you will begin to see differences between their reactions that will help you to form some assessment of their character.

From this very simple test, you will be able to tell a lot about the dog if you are patient and observant. Every behaviour has a motivation behind it, even if it is just a backward or forward step. It takes experience to guess accurately what the reasons behind behaviour may be, but everyone can guess. Once you have thought about why a dog may have behaved in a certain way, you can begin to make some assessment of his character and predict how he may behave in the future.

Carry out this test in a small kennel with a wire-mesh door where the dog sleeps or spends a lot of time. There should be no distractions such as people walking past or other dogs barking. If the dog is hungry, looking forward to a walk or has just seen his favourite member of the kennel staff, he will not pay you full attention and your assessment may be inaccurate. Remember to ensure the dog has been in the kennels for at least three days.

Reaction to strangers

When you first see a new dog, you will be a stranger to him so this is an ideal opportunity to test how friendly or otherwise he will be with strangers. Approach the dog in his kennel and crouch down in front of the door with your body sideways on and your eyes averted. Watch the dog's reactions. Does he approach in a friendly way, tail wagging? Does he come forward slightly, but look shy and hesitant? Does he give low growls or warning barks? Does he go to the back of the kennel and look worried? Does he begin to demand your attention by barking and pawing at the wire? Or he is more interested in the other dogs and whatever else is going on than in you?

A dog that readily comes forward to meet you is likely to do this to visitors to your home once he has settled in. A dog that is wary, but looks as though he wants to be friendly will probably be a very loyal watch-dog, but not necessarily one to take into a busy household. A dog that demands attention by barking or pawing at the wire has probably learned to do this in a previous home and will need careful retraining to eradicate the bad habit.

Once you have determined how the dog behaves towards strangers, swivel round to face him without getting up and talk to him in a friendly way through the bars. Spend a few minutes talking to him and again note his reaction.

Enjoyment of body contact

If you think it is safe to do so, put your fingers up against the bars, but don't put them inside to begin with. Does he press himself up against you so that he can be stroked? Dogs that enjoy being stroked will often shift sideways so they can press their whole body against the bars for maximum contact with you. Little dogs that are used to being picked up and cuddled will often bounce up and down excitedly at this point. Dogs that are more aloof will keep their distance. This could be through shyness, their lack of motivation to be touched or because they have not been stroked much in the past. Love and affection is often in short supply at rescue

This dog enjoys being stroked and has positioned herself so that it is easy for the person to touch her.

This dog feels uneasy and is licking his lips to try to stop someone staring at him.

kennels despite the attempts of dedicated staff, so if a dog does not respond to you at this stage and you want a dog that will enjoy lots of body contact, you may need to look elsewhere.

You may find that it takes a while for the dog to trust you enough to come forward to be stroked. If you are patient and are rewarded by the dog presenting his neck area to be touched, you will have found a dog that will be loyal and trusting with its owner, but aloof and reserved with strangers.

Hand-shy?

At this stage, you may like to judge his reaction to sudden hand movements. Dogs that have been smacked too much will either take evasive action or become aggressive. Raise your hand suddenly above the dog's eye level. A dog that has had no mistreatment will probably blink and then wag his tail. A dog that has been hit is likely to cower with his eyes closed, move away, or show aggression towards you. One that shows aggression to a suddenly raised hand is not likely to be safe around children. If you have children at home and the dog stiffens up and stares when you raise your hand suddenly, it may be worth repeating this movement several times to see if you can push it into using aggression. This may seem unfair to the poor dog, but it would be more unfair if he was to bite your children and had to be returned.

Afterwards talk to the dog kindly until he has relaxed and you have reassured him that your intentions are good.

Strength of character and sociability

Remove your hands and make eye contact with the dog. Observe his reaction. Does he stare back, look away quickly, retreat or show a range of submissive gestures, such as licking his lips? How he responds can tell you a lot about him.

In a dog's language, prolonged staring can be a threat of intended aggression. A dog that has been well socialised and is friendly and unafraid will have learned that human staring is safe and a signal to approach. If the dog you are assessing stares back at you with a happy expression and a wagging tail, it is a sign that he will get on well with most people.

Dogs that are less well socialised will avoid direct eye contact by looking away. Most dogs will do this. Staring may induce a sense of unease in the dog and he may yawn, suddenly become interested in something else, scratch or turn away and move to the back of the kennel. Some dogs may become aggressive with a warning growl, a display of teeth or sometimes, though rarely, an explosive display of anger. Through these responses, you will be able to see how the dog copes with a mild threat from a human and whether his future behaviour is likely to be suitable for you and your family.

Prolonged eye contact will often evoke signs of appeasement and submission in the form of lip licking or paw raising. If the dog displays extreme submission, such as rolling onto his back or continuous paw movements and wriggling soon after you begin to stare, he will probably have little confidence in his ability to deal aggressively with difficult situations, preferring instead to choose appeasement. Such a dog may be ideal for a family with children, but may not tolerate isolation from the safety of other pack members very easily.

Dogs with strong characters will often stare back at you if you stare at them. Dobermanns and rottweilers are renowned for this. They seem to weigh up your next move and have the confidence to hold their ground while under threat. This is an ideal characteristic for a guard dog. These dogs will often learn quickly and be quite independent. However, they may be more likely to react with aggression when seriously threatened and, unless you are sure about their past history, it may be better to avoid such dogs if you have children.

TIP

Staring and raising your hands quickly in front of a dog's face are very threatening to him and should be done only when he is safely behind bars. It is not pleasant for the dog being tested and you should do this only with dogs that you are genuinely interested in. If you have any doubts about the friendliness of the dog after your test, look elsewhere.

Trainability

It is possible to train all dogs, but some will learn faster than others. Offer the dog a titbit. If he takes it and eats it greedily, you can test him to see if he will be easy to train. Hold the next titbit just out of his reach and keep it still. He will probably sit down. As soon as he does something else to try to get the titbit, such as pawing at the wire or pressing his mouth to the bars, reward him immediately by feeding the titbit. Offer another in the same way and wait for the same behaviour to be shown before giving it to him. After a few repetitions, you will notice that the dog has worked out exactly what he has to do to get the titbit. Very smart dogs will learn after just a few attempts while it will take the less able longer.

Trainable dogs are also likely to be inventive about displaying behaviours that increase their chances of getting the titbit. If a dog just sits there waiting for a long time, he may be a very patient, steady dog who does not do the unexpected, but he will probably not be as smart as a dog that is constantly inventing novel behaviour.

Right: A titbit is held just out of reach. Be patient while the dog thinks of what to do.

Opposite: The dog raises a paw in an attempt to get the titbit. Give the titbit immediately and it is likely that he will repeat the behaviour next time.

Other traits to look for

Throughout the tests in part one, you will have seen how active or lazy a dog is. One that is constantly leaping up and down or pacing to and fro will be one that likes to be kept active. One that has only just enough energy to plod over to you and sit down may be quite happy to lie around all day while you get on with your life.

Other dogs in adjoining kennels will probably be barking or walking past during the assessment. Watch how the dog you are assessing reacts. Does he behave aggressively? If so, he is likely to behave like this to some other dogs in your environment once he has settled in. Is he more interested in other dogs than in you? If so, he may have grown up with other dogs and it may be difficult for him to become a human-oriented dog.

SIGNS TO WATCH FOR

Anxiety or uneasiness:
- Looking away
- Lip licking
- Ears held back
- Weight on back legs ready to run
- Growling

Appeasement:
- Lip licking
- Raised paw
- Rolling onto back

Once you have made an initial assessment, a member of staff will give you more information and will help you take the dog out of the kennel.

PART TWO

ASSESSMENT OUTSIDE THE KENNEL

Once you have found a dog or dogs that seem to have potential from your tests, the second part of this assessment procedure will help you decide which is your perfect rescue dog. You will need to take the dog out of the kennel so ask the permission of the kennel staff before doing so.

Taking an unknown dog out of his kennel always carries with it a slight risk. You will not know what treatment the dog received from strangers in the past and so you should proceed with caution. However, the kennel staff would be unlikely to allow you to take out a problematic dog. If you treat him with respect, handle him gently, take things slowly and do not expect too much of him at first, you are unlikely to experience problems. A dog cannot tell you if he is unhappy with something so watch for signs that he is anxious. Growling or lip curling signal the intention to bite so if either happens stop what you are doing at once. Do not try to discipline him, just accept that you took things too far with this particular dog too soon.

General observations

From the moment you begin to interact with the dog, you need to make observations that will help you build up a picture of his character. It is easy to get a lead on to his collar? Does he begin to bark frantically as soon as he knows he is going out? Does he leap up and down so much that it is difficult to calm him down enough to clip the lead on? Is he just very pleased to see you and not as interested in going out? Once out, does he pull hard on the lead and insist on going through doorways first (see page 70) All of these observations will help you assess the dog's character and predict its future behaviour.

Behaviour with other dogs

As you walk the dog out of the building, watch his interaction with other dogs. Does he try to avoid most dogs and hide behind you if another dog barks at him? Is he quite tolerant of other dogs barking at him, but cannot resist having a go back at the most ferocious? Does he keep his head down and try to get away from them as quickly as possible? Or is he aggressive to every dog that he comes across?

Kennels can be very hostile places as far as dog interactions are concerned. There are almost always a few dogs that do not like other dogs and these will bark and threaten the others as they go past. Such hostility can push even the most mild-mannered dog into self-defence and you will probably see your chosen dog behaving at his very worst in this environment.

If you have the opportunity to take him for a walk, take it. You will then be able to see how he interacts with other dogs when out

In the face of such an angry demonstration from the little dog, this big German Shepherd puts out his tongue and licks his nose to try to calm the aggression.

on walks. Does he ignore other dogs and concentrate on the walk or on the humans? Does he lunge aggressively at all dogs? Is he very keen to play and interact with other dogs? Aggression towards other dogs is usually caused by fear and most dogs can be brought out of it with patience (see pages 108 to 111). You may not have the time, commitment or experience to embark on such a project, so it is best to know in advance if there are any problems in this area.

While he is looking towards another dog, see if you can distract him with a tasty titbit or a game with a toy. If he cannot be distracted, walk away from the other dog and try again. How distracted he is will indicate how easy it will be to teach him to come back to you when he is out playing in the park and has become interested in other dogs.

Playing with toys

Once you have taken the dog out and given him some exercise, find an undisturbed place, preferably enclosed so that you can get to know him a bit better. Let him off the lead and allow him to explore the room or area for a while. Sit down quietly and wait for him to come to you. How long it takes will indicate how people-oriented he is and how much he enjoys their company.

This dog enjoys playing with toys and waits patiently for the toy to be thrown.

When he has settled down, produce a toy, tease him with it briefly in an excited way and throw it for him. Does he rush after it? Does he pick it up? Does he come back and drop the toy for you to throw again? If so, this indicates that chase is his favourite game and he is not a possessive dog. Dogs that play like this often make very nice pets. How obsessive about playing chase is he? If he plays for a long time and is still keen for more, you will need to think about whether you are prepared for this level of game playing on a regular basis.

Try to take the toy away from him. Does he growl or go rigid? If he does, it is not wise to proceed further unless you are very experienced. Does he tease you with the toy and hang on to it when you try to take it? Does he like to play tug-of-war? If he does, it may indicate a strong character. Try to get him really excited by rushing about and waving the toy wildly. Does he play gently or roughly after this? If you have children, especially small ones, this will be a useful exercise as it will tell you how careful he is with his teeth and how inhibited his biting is.

Encourage him to play with a squeaky toy. Does he back away from it or squeak it gently? Does he squeak it hard and try to tear it to pieces? Dogs that enjoy 'killing' squeaky toys often enjoy catching small animals. Their predatory instinct tends to be well defined – many of the terriers and hounds fall into this category. If you have a cat or other small pets at home and this dog enjoys 'killing' small, squeaky things, it may not be wise to choose him.

If the dog will not play, it could be that he does not know how to or it may be that he is not feeling relaxed enough to try. Give him more time to settle down and feel at ease. If he is still not playful, take special care to note how he behaves with other dogs. If he prefers their company to yours, it may be that he has been raised with another dog and has never had to learn to play with people. Such dogs can make good pets, but it takes a while to focus their attention onto people and to teach them to play properly.

This dog is comfortable about being handled and is happy and relaxed while being groomed.

Handling and grooming

Allow the dog to settle down again after the play session. Sit on the floor and encourage him to come closer. If he comes to you, stroke and handle him gently. If you feel it is safe to do so, run your hands gently over his body, down his tail and down each leg. Let him walk away if he wants to and watch for signs of unease such as yawning, ears back, the whites of the eyes showing and a lowered, still tail. Do not proceed if you see any of these signs. If he appears happy and relaxed, try gently restraining him and repeating the procedure. Finally, try some gentle brushing. If all goes well, try picking up each foot in turn and wipe them with a towel.

All of these procedures will allow you to judge how much the dog has been handled in the past and how comfortable he is with it. It will also enable you to assess how much he enjoys body contact. A dog that is not comfortable with handling and grooming can be brought round with care and patience, but such a dog may not be ideal to have around children unless they are very gentle and reserved.

This dog enjoys the company of children and remains calm and relaxed when they try to touch him.

Response to commands

When the dog is standing, ask him to sit. Most dogs know this command. How quickly does he respond? Does it take two or three repetitions? If he responds, praise him, encourage him to stand again and ask him to sit. Does he sit willingly and quickly a second time? And a third? If he understands the command, how willing he is to obey will give you an indication of his biddability. Many dogs will not respond well to someone they have yet to get to know, but the easy-going, responsive ones will.

Behaviour with children

Before taking any dog out with your children, question the centre staff closely about the information they have from previous owners. Try to make an estimate of how reliable this information may be based on your knowledge of the dog so far. Assessing whether a dog will be good with children is one of the most difficult things to do, which is why you need to rely on information from the previous owners.

Make sure your children are present throughout the assessment procedures so you can observe the dog's reaction to them and his friendliness towards them. Watching them play together with toys will give you further insight into the dog's suitability. If your handling and grooming exercises went well, you may like to allow your children to try some gentle brushing and see how the dog responds. Allow him to approach the children when he is ready and to move away if he wishes. An ideal dog for a family with children will tolerate all their attentions well and should appear to be enjoying them. If you have any doubts, it is probably better to go with your intuition.

If you have children, it would be unwise to consider stray dogs, those for which there is no background information or those that are known to be difficult around children. Sadly, many dogs will have been teased into being aggressive to children. These dogs would probably make very good pets if living with decent children, but it is wise to give them a miss and let them go to families of adults instead. If your children are older teenagers, you will not need to be so careful and you will have a wider choice than those families with younger children.

If you do not have children living at home, but have grandchildren or children who visit regularly, try to get them to visit the centre with you. If this is not possible, you will have to rely on previous information and the observations of the kennel staff who may have witnessed interactions with children.

Other factors to consider

There are many things you will not be able to tell from meeting the dog and the assessment procedure, such as how good a traveller he is. However, you will have a much better idea of his character after the assessment and this will enable you to predict future behaviour. For example, if he is nervous and seems scared by many things, it is likely that he will also be afraid of travelling in the car.

GOOD WITH SMALL ANIMALS?

One of the most difficult areas to find out about is how good the dog is likely to be with cats and other small animals. If you are lucky, the rescue centre will have a few worldly-wise cats about the place that can be used to gauge the dog's response. Unfortunately, these cats are used to dealing with unruly dogs and usually have so much confidence that new arrivals do not dare to tackle them. When faced with a cat that is preparing to flee, however, the same dog that turned away from the rescue centre cat will often take great delight in giving chase.

All you can really do is use the interactions to give you a general impression of the dog's excitability when faced with a cat. If he pays a great deal of attention to the centre cat and becomes very excited, especially if he is a terrier type or a hound, it may be best to avoid him if you have cats and other small animals. Ask the staff for their advice and try to find out if he lived with a cat in a previous home. An adult terrier or a greyhound/lurcher type who has not lived with cats before is not a good prospect. Some collies are so keen to chase that they can make life miserable for any cats they live with, but this does depend on the individual's character and how they have been brought up.

MEETING YOUR OTHER DOG(S)

Once you have chosen a dog, you will want to see if he can get along with any other dogs you may have. If there is a large open area at the rescue centre, get them together a few times before you decide to take the new dog home. The dogs will then be more familiar with each other before one has to move into the other's territory.

The worst way to introduce two dogs is head to head in a small space. The intensity of such a meeting can often result in a defensive display of aggression from one of the dogs. Instead,

'The worst way to introduce two dogs is head to head in a small space.'

When introducing your dog to a new dog, start off some distance apart and gradually get closer together. This will allow the two dogs to get used to each other slowly.

walk them in a large, open space in parallel with each other, keeping them apart initially. Keep walking so that the interest of the walk takes the pressure off the meeting. Gradually allow them to get together and interact with each other. Try to keep their leads as slack as possible so you are not influencing the body signals they give each other. If you are very lucky they will play together, but most dogs will ignore each other at this stage. Consider this a successful meeting as it will take them time to get to know each other – at least there was no fighting (see page 51).

Success at this stage, and on subsequent meetings, does not guarantee that the dogs will live happily together. They will still need to establish a hierarchy and this can be a source of friction between them. However, if they have been all right together during the first introduction, it is more likely that they will settle down eventually.

Taking on a challenge

In every rescue centre, there will be several dogs that need experienced owners. They will have difficult behaviour problems that need to be overcome. These dogs are incredibly rewarding to rehabilitate and there are some owners who take pleasure in taking a difficult dog and turning it into a decent member of society. It is possible to turn the majority of difficult dogs around, but it takes skill and experience to know which dog to choose. You run the risk of being heartbroken if you fail and the dog has to be returned or put to sleep. However, if you succeed, you will have the satisfaction of knowing that without your help that dog may not have survived. Such dogs are not ideal for first time owners, but the more experience you have, the more difficult a case you will be able to take on. Always consider the people you have contact with (family, friends and neighbours) before you take on a problem dog and get their agreement first.

This dog is large, lively and afraid of strangers. He will need experienced owners to help him overcome his fear and settle down.

CHAPTER

3

Early Days and Introductions

Arrange to collect your new dog in the middle of a weekend so you have just one day before everyone goes out to work or school and the everyday routine begins. If you spend a week at home to settle him in, he will get used to having you around all the time and will find it very difficult to cope when normal life resumes. Many dogs will sleep a lot during the first few weeks in a new house. Whether this is a reaction to stress or just because the dog is warm and comfortable and enjoying the luxury of being able to sleep all day is unclear, but if you take a week off work to be with him, he is likely to be quite unresponsive anyway.

Preparations

Before bringing your new dog home, everyone who will be looking after him should agree on the house rules that you will expect him to stick to. Decide whether he should be allowed upstairs, in the bedrooms, on the furniture or to be fed from the table. You also need to decide who is going to walk him, feed him, play with him and groom him?

Choose his name and draw up a list of commands you will use. If everyone uses the same words and keeps to the same rules it will be a lot less confusing for your dog and he will learn your house rules much more quickly. Decide also where he should sleep and, if you have young children, make it clear to them that he is not to be disturbed when he goes to lie there. The area around his bed should be a no-go zone for children so that he can be left alone if he needs rest.

Buy a good collar and a leather or nylon lead. Do not buy a chain or rope lead as this can hurt your hands and his neck. Buy toys, brushes and a bed. You should already know what kind of toys he likes and you will need brushes to suit his coat type. Do not buy an expensive bed at first in case he chews it. A strong cardboard box with the front cut down and a thick blanket inside will be fine to begin with and can be replaced with something more comfortable later.

The first day

How well your new dog travels in the car will probably be one of the first things you will find out about him unless you are walking home. If you are collecting him in a car, make sure whoever comes with you gets into the car first and put the dog in last. Start by placing him in the spot where you always intend him to travel so that he begins good habits straight away. Ensure he has got enough room and is not squashed in too tight with too many children. Fasten him or put up a barrier so that you do not have to start off by correcting him if he tries to jump into the front to join you. Ignore any bad behaviour in the car as this is something you will need to tackle later on (see pages 144 to 147).

Take him straight home (unless you have another dog, see page 49) and walk him into the garden. Let him off the lead to run around and explore. Sooner or later he will go to the toilet. It is worth waiting for him to do so, even if it is cold and wet outside. Praise him profusely as soon as he has been and feed him two or three small titbits while you do so. This will get him into a good habit from the beginning. When he needs to go to

Encourage your new dog to jump into the car if possible. If necessary lift him slowly and gently, holding him firmly in case he struggles.

Allowing your dog to explore the garden before going into the house will enable him to go to the toilet after the journey.

Tip

Make sure your new dog forms good habits straight away. Reinforce good behaviour by praising. Gently correct behaviour you do not approve of, but try not to shout or get angry.

the toilet again later, he will remember where he went and this will help to keep the house clean.

Once he has been to the toilet, or has made a thorough investigation of the garden, allow him inside to explore the house. From the moment he goes inside, begin to explain the house rules to him. He will not know what they are at first and may behave as he used to in his previous home. If he does something you do not wish him to do in your house, correct him quietly and calmly and gently show him what you want him to do instead. Try to make it clear that he has done something wrong, but do not sound angry or be too aggressive or he may become fearful and defensive, which will slow up the learning process. If he is shy or sensitive, be gentler with him so that you do not frighten him. As soon as he does something you approve of praise him warmly. In this way, he will quickly begin to learn what you expect of him.

After he has had about an hour to get used to the house, it may be a good idea to take him for a walk. He may have settled down enough to need to go to the toilet again and the pleasurable experience of walking with you will help him feel more at home. Take some toys with you as you may be able to entice him into a game that will help to get your relationship off to a very good start.

Remember, though, that he does not know you or your home. You cannot tell him that this is his new home and there is nothing he should worry about. He will feel displaced, unsure and unsettled for a while and you should try to ensure that he has the time and space he needs to adjust during that time. Try to be sympathetic to how he feels, but do not allow any bad habits to begin that you may later want to correct.

Introducing children

Your new dog will probably have met your children at the rescue centre, but first impressions of them at home are very important. If you left your children at home while you collected your new dog, they will be excited at the prospect of his arrival. It is essential that your dog is not crowded by the children or forced to interact with them until the excitement of being somewhere new has worn off.

It is probably best if the children are asked not to touch the dog while he is let into the garden. This will give him time to explore and to go to the toilet. Hold on to toddlers so they cannot suddenly rush forward towards the dog. Ask the children to go into the house first and sit down. Give them a few small dog food treats each and ask them to wait while he makes his initial exploration of the house. They can then call him one at a time, giving him one titbit on the flat of the hand when he goes to them.

Keep children restrained while your new dog explores the garden. If your dog is playful, a quick game with a toy will help settle him in and get rid of excess energy before going into the house.

Dogs will take to children more easily if they are sitting down, and if they stroke them on the chest rather than the head.

TEACH YOUR CHILDREN WHAT TO DO

Teach them in advance how to give food treats by placing it on their palm, keeping their fingers together, putting their hand down beneath the dog's mouth level and keeping it still. Also teach them how to stroke a dog safely by touching him under the chin and throat rather than by patting his head. Putting hands onto a dog's head covers up his sense organs and can be misconstrued as an aggressive act if the hands approach too fast. Be prepared to move the dog away if your child becomes overwhelmed or the dog is about to jump up. A big dog at face level may seem huge and can be a bit frightening.

Dogs do not always appreciate being hugged or cuddled unless they have been familiarised with it from an early age. It is very tempting for children to do this, especially if they have been used to hugging a previous dog. You will need to find out gradually what your dog will accept from the children, supervising constantly at first to ensure that neither is feeling overwhelmed by the actions of the other.

Once the initial introductions in the house have been made and the excitement has died down, this may be a good time to introduce a new game or toy for the children, which will keep them occupied and take their minds off the new arrival. This takes the pressure off your new dog who can then get to know the children in his own time.

Once everyone has had a chance to settle down and your new dog has had some rest, take them all out into the garden or out for a walk. Take the dog's toys out with you and try to get children and dog playing happily together. Eventually, both dog and children will need to learn certain rules if the games are to be successful (see page 48), but these initial games should be as much fun as possible for all concerned. Take a light-hearted approach and intervene only if the situation seems to be getting out of hand.

GO AT THE DOG'S PACE

For the first two weeks at least, insist that your children let your dog approach them rather than the other way around. They can call him to them if they want to, but should be taught not to go to him if he does not want to go to them. This will give him the time and space he needs to build his confidence with them. Keeping to this regime may be more difficult with younger children, but it will be your responsibility to ensure that they are constantly supervised so that no harm comes to either children or dog.

If your children have not had a dog before, they will need to be taught to respect him and not treat him as a toy. The high-pitched squeals of excited children can upset a dog until he is used to them, so try to keep play as calm as possible and

Titbits given on the flat of the hand help to give a good first impression.

interrupt it before it begins to get out of hand. Some dogs, such as collies, have a strong herding instinct and may nip at children's ankles when they run. This usually causes them to squeal and run away, which excites the dog more. Be ready to step in at once to stop the behaviour, which will otherwise quickly become a habit.

LEARNING THE BASICS

Children have to learn not to tease or bully your dog; the dog has to learn not to jump up, be too boisterous or nip them in play. It is important to supervise all their activities until they have both learned the rules. It is not advisable to leave children under the age of 10 alone with any dog. Until you are sure that your new dog does not guard its food from children, it would be wise to give him bones and chews when they are in bed or put him into another room that can be locked to ensure that young children do not wander in unexpectedly. Teach your children never to approach a dog when it is eating or chewing a bone or chew.

Follow the same rules and procedures for introducing any visiting children to your dog. If your dog has a pleasant first encounter with them, if he is not crowded by them or approached when he wants to be left alone and if he sees them as a source of titbits and games he will begin to enjoy having them around and they will soon become friends (unless he has been badly frightened by children in his past).

BE VIGILANT

If you do not have children and you have chosen a dog that has an unknown history with them, you will need to proceed cautiously when any children visit or if you meet any outside the home. It is safer to assume that your new dog is not good with children until you have had time to observe his reactions to them. If you are still unsure, it may be wise to muzzle him to begin with. This will tend to make him a little more fearful if he was afraid to begin with, but it will prevent him biting. Make sure that your dog is used to the muzzle beforehand (see page 104) so he does not associate it with the presence of children.

CHILDREN

- Make sure children don't overwhelm your new dog.
- Let the dog approach the children rather than the other way around.
- Teach children how to give titbits safely.
- Teach children how to stroke a dog properly.
- Buy your children a new game or toy to take the attention from your new dog.

Give the two dogs time to get to know each other in the garden, where there is more space and the desire to 'defend the territory' is less strong.

Introducing other dogs

If you are taking your new dog home by car, keep him separate from your existing dog. Try to find an area that is unfamiliar to both dogs on the way home where there is plenty of space for their first walk together. The interest of the walk will make the introduction less intense and they can get to know each other as they walk. Keep them walking in parallel and try to avoid head to head encounters. Walk them for as long as possible, gradually letting them have more and more contact with each other. Don't worry if they ignore each other at this stage.

After the walk, when they are both well exercised, take them home and let them both into the garden. If your new dog is shy and you have more than one existing dog, take it in turns to let each dog meet the new dog so that he does not get overwhelmed.

Before allowing them into the house, remove anything they are likely to fight over such as toys, bones, beds and bowls. Allow time for the new dog to explore the house and then separate them while any children are introduced. If you are using titbits, take the new dog out of the room once he has met all of the children and allow the existing dog back in to get some treats. Make sure all the food has gone before the two are let back in together so there is nothing to fight over.

ESTABLISHING A HIERARCHY

Try to ignore any small disagreements or scuffles between the two dogs at first. If you see both dogs stiffening up and staring at each other, distract them by pretending something much more interesting is going on elsewhere. If they look as though they may fight, attach short leads to their collars so you can use these to break up an incident. If a fight ensues, do not grab at the dogs to break it up as you may get bitten by accident or make the fight worse. Use the leads to part them or a sudden surprise, such as throwing a bucket of water over them, banging tin trays together loudly just above their heads or throwing a heavy coat over them. Afterwards, be ready to lead each dog away and isolate them until they have calmed down.

Usually, introductions go smoothly and the new dog is treated, and acts, like a visitor. The hierarchy between them is usually sorted out during the first few weeks and disagreements are possible during this time. Try to avoid situations that may cause aggravations between the two. Feed them separately, for example, until they are used to each other and do not make such a fuss of the new dog that the existing dog feels excluded. Take care not to leave them alone together until it is obvious they have become friends.

Dogs that live together will always form a hierarchy. Initially, the existing dog will be leader of the pack and it is important that you, as the owner, is seen to reinforce this. This means treating them not as equals, but instead favouring your existing dog by putting him first in most things, such as feeding, giving attention, playing and going through doorways. This should be easy as you will have a stronger bond with him anyway.

Gradually over the following two weeks the dogs will make their own assessment of who should be in charge. If the new dog is mentally stronger and more ambitious, he may well end up taking over. This could happen without any problems or the existing dog could resist which may lead to scuffles and fights. Try not to interfere in this natural process unless they begin to fight. If it becomes obvious that the new dog has taken control, you will have to reinforce this by putting the new dog first in everything instead. This may be difficult to do, particularly if your sympathies lie with your first dog. However, not to do this will interfere in the natural pack order and could lead to fights between the dogs.

Be particularly careful not to do anything that may aggravate a situation between your dogs during the settling-in period. Shut

Opposite: Attaching a long line to your dog's collar when he is in the presence of your cat will enable you to stop him quickly should he decide to give chase.

them into two separate rooms when you give them chews and bones and take the treats away before they are allowed back together. Be careful with them at moments of excitement such as when you are about to take them out for a walk, if someone has returned home, if the doorbell rings or the postman delivers letters. This is a time when annoyance with each other is likely to flare into a fight. If they are small dogs, be particularly careful not to lift one above the other and, in doing so, unwittingly give the underdog a height advantage that can trigger the top dog into aggression.

Not all dogs fit in well to a life with other dogs. Dogs that have been doted on by previous owners, for example, may be too obsessive about their humans to allow any other dogs near. Watch out for signs of bullying by the strongest dog. If, after one month, either dog is very unhappy with the situation or there are often fights and scuffles between them and the situation is not getting better, it may be kinder to let the new dog go to another home.

BREAKING UP A DOG FIGHT

- Never attempt to separate fighting dogs with your hands.
- If the dogs are wearing leads, use these to separate them.
- Try to defuse the situation by throwing water or a heavy coat over them.

Introducing cats

Cats and dogs living in the same household can become friends and enjoy each other's company. How you introduce them and how they take to each other on the first few meetings is critical for future success. It is essential that your cat does not become frightened of the dog or the dog learns that it can chase the cat. If

Allow the cat to come and go as it pleases but ensure that the dog is restrained so that he cannot give chase.

either of these things happen, the time taken for them to live happily together will be greatly extended.

It is best to shut the cat away upstairs or in a different room while the dog comes in and explores the house. The two animals will quickly become aware of each other's presence because of their keen sense of smell. Wait until all excitement has died down and the dog has had a chance to recover from all the new experiences. It may be better to wait until the evening when everyone is more relaxed and younger children are in bed.

Put the dog on his lead, sit down with him at the opposite end of the room to the door and wait until the dog is lying down and relaxed. Get another family member to let the cat out and encourage it to come into the room adjacent to where the dog is. Once the cat is in this room, ask someone to shut the doors so that the cat can only be in this room and the room where the dog is. Encourage it to come in to the room where the dog is by tempting it with food, but do not force things at this stage. Keep the dog as still as possible, insisting that it sits or lies down.

The cat is more likely to be brave if it feels it has an escape route or it can get up high. Your cat will not put itself in a dangerous situation that it cannot get out of. It needs to learn that the dog is safe before it can come closer so be patient and let things take a natural course. The more shy the cat and the more boisterous or vocal the dog, the longer it will take. Forcing things at this stage will result in more fear in the cat that will take longer to overcome. If your cat is bold or used to dogs, he may come straight in. If he begins to approach the dog, let the dog get up and greet the cat, but hold on to his collar just in case.

How many attempts it will take will depend upon the two animals in question. Keep the dog under complete physical control until there is no excitement generated by the cat's arrival. You can then gradually begin to allow the dog more freedom, but be sure you can prevent any chasing should it arise. Leave a trailing line on the dog that you can stand on in a hurry should a chase begin. This is a useful way of getting control quickly, but be careful with this if you have small children or elderly people in the house.

Ensure you supervise all encounters between your dog and cat for several weeks. They will get to know each other at their own speed. Sometimes it can take many months. Only by being in control of the meetings and by being calm and patient will you enable their friendship to develop as quickly as possible. Never leave them alone together until it is obvious that they are happy with each other.

If your cat is very timid, it may be wise to confine him to the house for the first week to prevent him running away when the dog arrives and refusing to come back. Lock the cat flap and give your cat an area of the house where the dog cannot go, such as upstairs. Put a litter tray in a convenient place and feed the cat somewhere away from the dog's territory so that it can eat undisturbed. This will enable the cat and dog to co-exist comfortably in the same house until you have the time to supervise their encounters.

Introducing smaller pets

Keep your new dog away from smaller pets for a few days until you have had time to develop a stronger bond with him. This will make him more responsive to you and he is more likely to take notice when you try to teach him how to behave around small, delicate animals. Small, active, fluffy or furry animals usually bring out the predatory instinct in the most placid of dogs. Some dogs have a stronger instinct than others do and certain types of dog, such as terriers and lurchers, are more likely to respond unfavourably.

Throughout all early introductions, keep your dog on a lead, under control and confine the small pet to its familiar cage. Allow the dog to approach slowly, but do not allow the small pet to be frightened. This is unfair and it may cause it to run, which will make your dog more excited. Insist that your dog sits or lies down. Talk calmly to your dog and praise him if he remains still. Be aware of things

Keep a new dog restrained and under close observation until you have seen how he behaves with small pets. A terrier and a rat is not a good combination.

The instinct to chase is very strong in many dogs. Quick, erratic movements of smaller pets can prove irresistible.

TIP

Before leaving your dog alone in the house, make sure small animals in cages are well out of reach or behind a secure door.

going on around you as any sudden excitement, such as a child running towards you, may cause your dog suddenly to lunge forward. Take time to allow your new dog to get used to the small pet, but end the session after about five minutes. Repeat as often as you can for the first week, taking care never to allow your dog to rush up to any cage.

You can repeat this procedure with the dog fastened securely while you handle the small pet. Again, insist that he sits or lies down. Get someone to help you to do this if necessary. By doing this, you will be able to gauge your dog's reaction to small creatures. Predatory dogs will become interested whenever the small animal moves, despite being given time to become familiar with them. Dogs that are scared and unfamiliar with small animals will gradually become used to them over time and, eventually, should take little notice of them. Whatever the reaction, remember that a dog's instincts often lie just below the surface and never put your dog in a position where he can grab at the smaller pet should it decide to make a sudden, unexpected movement.

The first night

It is a good idea to put your new dog to bed half an hour before going to bed yourself for the first few nights. This allows him to get used to the idea of being alone while your reassuring presence is nearby. It also allows you to judge how well he is likely to cope with the isolation. Make sure he has had a chance to go out to the toilet before putting him to bed.

If your dog is in any way pushy or strong-willed, insist that he stays in the kitchen at night and ignore all his attempts to get you to go back in to him. If you do so you will be rewarding his behaviour and it is likely to increase in intensity. Warn the neighbours that there may be a few sleepless nights and put something up against the door and over the carpet near the door so that he cannot damage it if he scratches while attempting to get out. Go into the room in the morning only if your dog is quiet. If you go in when he is barking, your appearance will reward his behaviour and he is likely to wake you up earlier in future. Wait until there is a pause in the noise before going in.

If your dog has a shy, gentle or submissive nature, you may find that he copes with his first few nights better if he can sleep closer to you. Put his bed outside your bedroom and close the door so he cannot disturb you in the night. You may hear him sniffing underneath the door during the night as he tries to reassure himself that you are still there.

If your new dog wakes up during the night and makes frantic attempts to attract your attention, he may want to go to the toilet. Get up and take him out, but do not speak to him or make a fuss of him. If you do, he will probably try to get you up again next time he is feeling a bit lonely. Wait with him in the garden until he has relaxed, and praise him if he does anything. If he doesn't go, bring him back in and leave him alone for the rest of the night. Once he has settled in and his body adjusts to your routines, these nightly exercises should disappear. (See page 135 for how to solve the problem of dogs that persistently have 'accidents' at night.)

Gentle or shy dogs may prefer to sleep closer to you at night. Putting a bed outside the bedroom door will help to settle him and to teach him that he cannot come into your room.

The early days of life together

After the first day with your new dog, introduce your house rules and continue with your normal daily routines as if your dog is already part of the family. Start as you mean to go on and your dog will adapt more quickly to your lifestyle. In particular, make sure you leave him alone in the house for a period of time on each of the first few days. This will have to happen eventually and he is more likely to accept it if it happens straight away. Rescue dogs are renowned for getting very attached to new owners very quickly and you may find it becomes impossible to leave him if you do not get him used to it at once. How long you leave him for will depend on the character of the dog. Shy, gentle, submissive dogs usually find it harder to cope without you. This is especially important if you go out to work. He will quickly get used to your routines and to being left and will see it as a bonus when you are around rather than becoming anxious whenever you cannot be with him. See chapter 8 for how to teach your dog to be left alone.

During the first few days of your new life together, try to introduce him to people outside your immediate family who will be visiting often. Relatives and close friends should be encouraged to visit so they can meet your new dog. Anyone he meets often during these early weeks is likely to be treated as part of your extended pack and will be greeted accordingly.

Do not keep him isolated during this time, particularly if he is shy, as this is likely to make him insular and suspicious of anyone outside his immediate family. Try to ensure that he enjoys his encounters with new people. Give them titbits to give him, or toys to throw for him. Let him approach them rather than the other way around and watch his body language for signs of stress. If he is too boisterous, keep him on a lead while he greets people so you can control his actions. Allow him to go forward only when he is behaving sensibly and not jumping up.

BATHING

A good rescue centre will ensure that your new dog has been bathed prior to you picking him up. If, for some reason, he has not been bathed and he is very smelly, it may be best to wait for a few days before washing him rather than add to the stress he is already under. When the time comes, lift him into a dry bath or shower tray onto a non-slip mat and add water afterwards. He will then be less likely to panic and splash water everywhere than if you try to put him into a full bath. Talk to him quietly to reassure him while you are washing him, and dry him thoroughly with a towel afterwards.

Insist on good manners from day one when greeting visitors.

HOUSE-TRAINING AND THE IMPORTANCE OF ROUTINES

During the early days with your new dog, try to stick to a schedule for feeding, walking and sleeping. This will help your dog adjust more quickly to your routines and will help him readjust his body from the routine he was used to in kennels.

Until he has had time to adjust, leave newspaper on the floor by the back door whenever you leave him so that he can go to toilet on this if necessary. Place polythene underneath the newspaper to prevent any leakage on to the floor. This is important as dogs have such a strong sense of smell, which will attract them back to use the same place next time.

Leaving your new dog alone for short periods during the first few days will help him learn to accept isolation.

Most adult dogs will have been house-trained, but some may have been in kennels for a long time and may need reminding. Take your dog outside to the garden on numerous occasions and on regular walks during the first few days to remind him of the right place to go (see page 136 for advice on house-training problems). When taking him to the garden, make sure you stay with him for reassurance and so you can praise him and let him know he has been good when he goes to the toilet.

Your dog is likely to be excited and slightly anxious during the first few days of his new life. This may cause his immune system to be depressed and may allow any minor ailments that his body was just coping with in kennels to come to the fore. Your dog may develop loose bowels, which may cause him to have house-training accidents. Try not to be upset by this or react adversely towards your dog. Clean up the soiled area with biological washing powder solution or special products available from your veterinary practice. Many other household cleaning products will not remove all of the smell and your dog may be attracted back to the area. Do not let symptoms persist for longer than 24 hours before consulting a veterinary surgeon.

You can reduce the chances of your new dog developing diarrhoea by acquiring at least a week's supply of the food your dog was eating in kennels so that you can implement any dietary changes slowly. The last thing your dog needs when he is adjusting to his new home is changes happening inside his body as his system adjusts to the new food. If you want to change your dog's diet, make changes slowly once he has settled into the family by gradually increasing the proportion of new food to old over a few days.

During the first few days, accompany your dog when he goes out to the garden to go to the toilet.

CHAPTER

4

Building a Successful Relationship

All good relationships are based on trust and friendship. Your dog has to learn that you will do what is best for him and to trust you. This can be particularly difficult for dogs that have had a rough time with their first owners. In a similar way, you have to learn to trust that your dog will not bite you under any circumstances. This will take time and you will need to have many experiences together before you can both be really sure of your ground. The less you resort to punishment to get your own way and the fewer times you get angry with your new dog, the quicker he will learn to trust you.

If he is the right dog for you and you take time to understand him and treat him well, a strong bond of friendship will gradually grow between you. You cannot expect this to happen overnight, but the more reasonable your behaviour is towards your dog, and the better you understand him, the quicker it will happen. Don't expect miracles too soon. It takes about six months for a dog to really settle down in a new home, for you to get to know him and all his faults, and for him to learn about you. While you should be able to develop a good working relationship long before this, it is likely to take quite a while before he is truly your dog.

As well as trust and friendship, a dog needs to have firm guidelines on what is acceptable behaviour and what is not. As long as he knows his boundaries and the ground rules of life with you, he can be free to be himself and to have fun without overstepping the mark. When your new dog comes home with you for the first time, he will have his own rules for life with humans based on his previous experiences. These rules are unlikely to be the same as yours and so you will need to be prepared to teach him a new set of boundaries from day one. How you treat him in the first six months will set the scene for the rest of your time together. Getting it right from the outset will be easier than backtracking later.

'Don't expect miracles too soon. It takes about six months for a dog to really settle down in a new home, for you to get to know him and all his faults, and for him to learn about you.'

Setting ground rules

It is important that you show your dog what is required from him and reward him for showing the correct behaviour. So often owners chastise or punish new dogs for breaking their rules, but as a new dog will have no idea that he is doing something wrong, this comes as a surprise to him and he can begin to resent and distrust his new owners if it happens too often. A much better way to train your dog is to try to anticipate and prevent any unwanted behaviour. If you know he was allowed on furniture in

Provide your dog with a suitable place for resting and teach him to go there when he is sleepy.

HOW DOGS LEARN

- Dogs learn by trial and error. If they are rewarded for doing something, they are more likely to do it again. If their actions bring no success, they are less likely to repeat them.
- A dog needs to be rewarded as soon as he does a required action. Although he can remember earlier actions, he cannot associate praise or correction with an action unless it follows immediately. Consequently, if you want your dog to continue to do what it is he is doing, praise and reward him for it at once and it is more likely to happen in future.

his first home, for example, attach a lead to his collar before you let him into your lounge so you can prevent him from jumping on the sofa. When he is looking for a place to settle, tap the carpet or his bed and encourage him to lie there instead. Reward him well for lying in the right place.

In the early days, remember to reward him whenever you catch him being good so he knows he is doing the right thing. It is easy to forget to do this when everything is going well, but it will help to let him know that you are pleased with him and will give a sharp contrast to times when you may need to correct him. If you make sure that good behaviour is rewarded, it will soon become a habit. Extreme unwanted behaviours, such as jumping up at small children, should be stopped at once. Take hold of your dog's collar and tell him off. Then immediately lighten your tone and show him how you want him to behave instead. As soon as he does this, praise and reward him.

What's in a name?

Strays or dogs that have not had good relationships with people will not know their name. Test whether your new dog knows his by waiting until he faces away from you and saying his name clearly, but quietly. If he responds, it is likely that he has learned to associate the sound of his name with pleasant experiences with humans and you may like to continue to use it, particularly if he is an older dog. If, however, he does not have these associations or looks worried when you say his name, it may be a good idea to change it, particularly if you do not like it very much.

Choose a name that is easy to say and that all family members will be happy to yell loudly in a public place. What you choose is not important, but there is a theory that the name you choose indicates the type of relationship you want from your dog. Calling the dog a human name such as Ben or Sally, for example, indicates that you want a closer relationship than if you choose Fido or Mutt. Use the new name as soon as you get your dog and make sure everyone calls him the same thing. Often names get shortened or lengthened, but it will be quicker for him to learn if you all keep to the same name for a while.

You can speed up the process by saying his name often whenever he is looking the other way or concentrating on something else and producing a titbit or playing a game whenever he looks at you. He will quickly begin to link the sound of his new name with something very pleasant and will begin to respond and orientate towards whoever calls him. If you use his name too often, however, or you are cross with him when you call him, he will steadily become more and more unresponsive.

Calling your dog's name and seeing how he responds is a good test of the relationship between you. If he responds happily and comes to you wagging his tail, he has a good relationship with you. If he ignores you or looks worried, you will need to work harder to gain his affection and confidence.

The 'honeymoon' period

During the first two weeks, your dog is likely to feel like a visitor and behave extraordinarily well. Try not to be taken in by this best behaviour – it is likely that there is bad behaviour to come. As your dog begins to see the home as his territory and the family as his pack, his confidence level will rise and you are likely to see behaviours appearing that were not present at first. Some of these behaviours, such as guarding the house or being less

It may take up to two weeks before your new dogs feels that he belongs to the territory and that he needs to defend it.

responsive to commands, may be unwanted. It is for this reason that rescue societies usually receive requests for advice approximately two weeks after adoption.

Be aware that this 'honeymoon' period occurs and have realistic expectations otherwise you may be very disappointed when your perfect dog turns out to have a bad side after all. If you have been warned of possible problem behaviours this period also gives you a chance to put in some work with the problems before your dog becomes confident enough to assert himself. For example, a shy dog may not bark or be aggressive for the first two weeks. This gives you time to socialise him and make him feel more comfortable with people so that, hopefully, he will view them in a different light by the time he has developed sufficient confidence to be difficult with them.

Some very confident dogs may settle down more quickly. Dogs that were never corrected or suppressed in their first home may walk in as if they own the place and take control of the situation immediately. However, other dogs may take more time, particularly those that were badly treated in their previous home. Dogs that were kept very suppressed or were ill or under-nourished in their previous home may take months before they find their feet and gain confidence.

Why is hierarchy so important to dogs?

All domestic dogs have descended from wolves – creatures that live in a structured society governed by a strong hierarchical system. The animals at the top of the pack get access to more resources than their subordinates and they are ones who will produce the puppies. In an established hierarchy pack members rarely need to fight – most pack members know their place and are careful not to overstep the mark. This ensures that injuries are minimised and they are all fit to help each other hunt.

This natural hierarchy system has been passed down via genes from their ancestors to our domestic dogs. The ambition to be pack leader will be stronger in some dogs than others and it will have been encouraged to different degrees in the dog's previous home. Until you are sure about your dog's view of the world from a hierarchical perspective, it may be best to assume that he

Only high ranking wolves produce puppies and pass on their genes to the next generation. This is a privilege lower ranking wolves do not have.

Wolves have a natural hierarchy system that has been passed down via their genes to our domestic dogs.

needs to be firmly placed at the bottom of the pack. Doing this from day one will ensure that you achieve your goal to become his pack leader. Leaving it a few weeks until you have found out how strong-willed he is will make it much harder to regain control once you have lost it. It is easier to relax the pressure that keeps him at the bottom of the pack if you find he does not need it, rather than apply pressure to him if he thinks he has the upper hand.

BEING A GOOD PACK LEADER

A dog that thinks he is pack leader will make his own decisions, will be out of control and, in general, will act like a spoilt child who will try all manner of things to get his own way. He will not obey commands or do anything he does not want to and will always want to be the centre of attention.

If you are pack leader, you will have the right to make decisions that affect members of your pack and your dog will have enough respect to abide by those decisions. Dogs that think they are at the bottom of the pack will be compliant and biddable. They will be under your control because they view you as a parental figure rather than as a slightly older brother or sister or, worse, a younger sibling.

No one can afford to have a dog that is out of control. Life in the house with a dog that thinks he is the boss is no joke. A well-behaved, obedient dog is a pleasure to own and is usually much happier than one that is in constant conflict with its owners.

YOUR RESPONSIBILITIES AS PACK LEADER

As a pack leader, it will be your responsibility to make decisions about who does what and when, including sorting things out when they go wrong, protecting the pack and making sure everyone is comfortable and happy. As your dog's pack leader, you are taking on total responsibility for his welfare. This means you have a duty to understand him, to find out what makes him feel happy and safe and to learn how he thinks and sees the world.

The best pack leaders are benevolent and tolerant, but can be tough when they need to be. You should make it clear you will stand no nonsense, but are happy to be the dog's friend. A good pack leader does not constantly bully the dog to force him to stay inferior. Once your dog understands who is in charge, he will be more than happy to accept his position in life. In fact, dogs who have had the responsibility of pack leadership taken off their shoulders are usually more puppy-like and playful.

The dog you take on will have a predetermined view of humans based on his previous experiences with them. Despite this view, how he is treated during the first few weeks in a new home will make a considerable impression on him. From the very first encounters with members of his new pack, he will be assessing them to find out where his position lies.

Winning a small contest, such as who will get out of the gate first, can help to prevent challenges over larger issues.

THE RIGHT ATTITUDE

It is important to show your dog that you are fit to be a pack leader and to resolve to will win contests and challenges with your new dog, however small these challenges are. If you are a gentle, easy-going person, you may need to steel yourself to be strong for the first few weeks while your dog settles in and learns your strengths. It is important that you manage all encounters well during this time. Ultimately, you cannot fool your dog forever, but you may be able to do so for long enough to get the upper hand. This is why it is so important to choose the dog with a character most suited to you (see Chapters 1 and 2).

Consider a situation where you meet a friend in the street and stop to talk to them. Your dog notices a lamp post close by that he wants to

investigate and he tries to pull you towards it. If you give in and allow him to move, he has got his own way and you have lost a small contest. If, however, you make him sit and wait until you have finished talking, then allow him to go there as a reward for his good behaviour, you have won the contest and increased your status in the dog's eyes. Insisting on good behaviour is all important. Winning small contests like this from the outset will help to ensure your dog does not try to challenge you over the bigger issues.

While establishing yourself as leader, do not issue commands that you are not in a position to enforce should your dog decide to ignore them. Nothing will lower your status quicker than your dog learning that he does not have to respect your wishes. If your dog ignores your first command, manoeuvre him gently, but firmly, into place before rewarding. Do not give four or five commands that he ignores, which makes you so angry you feel you want to punish him. Punishing a dog will not accelerate your promotion to pack leader status. The respect has to be earned and you will not increase your chances if you bully your dog. Dogs that are punished in an effort to train and dominate them are likely to react by becoming defensively aggressive.

THE NATURAL WAY TO ACHIEVE PACK LEADER STATUS

The easy way to achieve status as pack leader is to use the techniques that wolves use for maintaining their hierarchies. This is a natural way and one that dogs seem to understand instinctively. The techniques centre on situations and events on which your dog will place more significance than you. These are sleeping places, territory and movement of the pack around the territory; winning of games and possession of toys; order of feeding; and attention and grooming from other pack members.

Sleeping place and territory

The dominant wolves in a pack will choose the best den in the territory to raise their puppies. They will also choose the best places to rest and will move others out of their chosen spot if necessary. Movements around the territory are instigated by the dominant animals. In your house, you have chosen the bedrooms as the best places to sleep. If you allow your dog to sleep on your bed, you will encourage him to think that he is on an equal footing with you. Ambitious dogs should sleep in their own bed away from the bedrooms. You will also rest on

Leading the way helps your dog realise you are the one that makes the decisions.

Preventing your dog from going into your bedroom keeps him off the bed and gives you a higher status.

sofas and chairs. Allowing him on these will raise his status. It is best to keep ambitious dogs off the furniture. It is also a good idea to control movements of your dog around the territory/home by going through doorways, up stairs and through narrow openings first. Leaders should lead, followers should follow. This also prevents your dog charging ahead and dragging you through doorways and down steps at speed.

Playing to win

In the wild, the stronger animals are those that are able to maintain their positions at the top of the hierarchies. To be an 'alpha wolf', you need to be both physically and mentally strong. As a subordinate, your dog will depend on you, his pack leader, for leadership and protection – no one wants to be led by a weak leader.

Tug-of-war games are a trial of strength between dog and owner. During such games, both players find out who is physically and mentally stronger. The individual who wins most of the time is the one who, in the dog's eyes, is the best equipped to lead the pack. If your dog enjoys these games, it is important that you win more often than not. If you cannot win because your dog is too strong for you, it is better not to play possession games at all. Playing and losing will give an ambitious dog the wrong message.

Always take a toy away from your dog at the end of a play session. This will make you seem like a possessive animal and will give you higher status. If your new dog hides under tables or races round and round so that you cannot get the toy back, attach a long line to his collar before you play so that you can pull him over and remove the toy from him. If it is difficult to get the toy out of his mouth, hold a tasty titbit under his nose so that he drops the toy to eat the titbit. As he begins to let go, give him a 'leave!' command so he begins to associate the action of letting go with this command.

If you find that your new dog is stealing items and running away with them to challenge you, attach the long line again and deliberately leave things down for him to steal. When he does so, pick up the end of the line, ask him to come to you and use the line to enforce your command. Continue to pull him to you until you can remove the object he has stolen from his mouth. Put it back where he found it. Repeat if necessary and, sooner or later, your dog will realise that there is no advantage in trying to challenge you by stealing things because you always win.

'Always take the toy away from a strong-willed dog at the end of a play session. This will make you seem like a possessive animal and will give you higher status.'

Playing to win will help a strong-willed dog to learn that you can take control of the possession in the territory if you want to.

Order of feeding

In the wild, the dominant animals will usually eat first, keeping others away until they have had enough. This helps to ensure that the biggest, strongest animals stay fit and healthy in times of famine.

In your household, dogs should be fed after the rest of the family has eaten. This may seem relatively unimportant to you, but for many pet dogs feeding is one of the highlights of their day and it can be very significant.

Attention and grooming from other pack members

Dominant wolves will decide when they wish to have attention from their subordinates. At other times they will remain aloof and independent. In order to maintain high status with an ambitious dog, humans in the pack should initiate most of the interactions with him, rather than the other way around. Do not always respond to your dog's demands for attention.

Grooming your dog helps to strengthen the bond between the two of you and teaches him to accept being held and handled.

If you choose to ignore him, do not speak to him, look at him or touch him so that he gets the message. When he has gone away to lie down, call him to you and give as much affection as you like. Being aloof with a pushy dog helps him get the message that he is lower in status and helps to foster a more independent attitude in a dog that is likely to become over-attached to his new owners.

GROOMING

It is important for your dog to accept being touched, handled and groomed all over. Some dogs will not have learned to cope with this and will need to be familiarised with it gradually. Dogs that are happy with human contact will be more trusting and are more likely to allow veterinary attention, even with un-comfortable procedures. If you cannot handle your own dog without a struggle, your veterinary surgeon will not be able to either.

Try to groom your dog every day for the first few weeks. Even short-coated dogs need to accept being touched all over and it gives you a chance to do a quick health check at the same time. Keep sessions short at first and follow them up immediately with a treat, game or walk so your dog will learn that if he stands still and tolerates the attention he will be well rewarded.

If your dog is afraid, take things very slowly at first, brushing 'safe' areas such as down his back and on his shoulders. Work up to brushing underneath and between his hind legs. Some dogs have a very low pain threshold and tugging long hair or digging brushes into their skin can distress them. Previous rough handling may have made them terrified of brushes. It is important to persevere with such dogs and to work slowly and gently to gain their trust.

Some dogs will not let you groom them because they consider themselves too high in status. For dogs that try to wriggle away when they have had enough, who try to turn it into a game, try to bite the brush or nibble your fingers, insist on grooming until you have finished. Keep going until your dog gives in and allows you to groom him without making a fuss. Then break off and offer a big reward. It may be easier to place such a dog on a table where he will have less confidence. Put the table in the corner of a room so that you only have to prevent him from jumping off on two sides. Hold his collar with one hand and groom with the other. If there is too much resistance you may need to tie him. Ask a professional groomer to show you how to restrain a difficult dog.

KEEP FRINGES TRIMMED

If your dog jumps when you touch him on his side or back, it may be because he cannot see well as he has long hair covering his eyes. Sudden movements or touches that seem to come out of the blue could cause him to snap in self-defence. If your dog has a long fringe, carefully clip the hair from this area or tie it up out of the way. It may look less appealing but it is much more pleasant for your dog to be able to see where he is going.

Parents should always be on hand to help out if the dog likes to play tug-of-war.

For a pushy, self-confident dog, it is important to have complete physical control in case he behaves badly and continue grooming until he has accepted it.

If you groom your dog a little every day, even the most difficult dog will become more compliant and trusting. Continue to build this up gradually until you can look at his teeth, in his mouth, in his ears, lift up his legs and hold his paws. Do not overwhelm him with too much at first, but gradually introduce these exercises as he learns to trust you.

High status for children

It is important that your new dog learns that his position in the pack lies below that of any children in the family. Make sure that your children follow the guidelines given above, especially during the early days with your new dog. Do not allow them to sneak the dog up to their bedroom, either to sleep or play, until you are satisfied that the dog will not attempt to take over. Feed the children before the dog and keep him away from toddlers while they are eating to prevent him from stealing food from their hands. Encourage your children to join in the grooming process, but wait until your dog completely accepts being groomed and touched by all adults in the house first.

For dogs that enjoy tug-of-war games, ensure that an adult is on hand at all times to help a child win if necessary, especially if the child is small and your dog is big. If your dog feels that the family forms a coalition at such times to assist the children, he will feel that he cannot win against them and will consider himself lower than they are in the pack. If your dog is rough during play, avoid such games altogether when the children are present and play chase games instead.

CHAPTER 5

Understanding Your Dog's Needs

Dogs are usually able to fit into our families extremely well and it is sometimes easy to overlook the fact that they are from a completely different species. They view the world differently from humans, have a different way of communicating with each other and have different motivations for the things they do. If your dog is to behave well, it is important that you understand these differences and make allowances for them during interactions with him. Providing for his special species needs will ensure that he does not behave badly in an attempt to fulfil innate urges.

Dogs gather as much information by sniffing as we do by looking. Deposited scents around this post seem irresistible.

A world full of scent

When we go into a new situation, we use our eyes to gather information about what is happening around us; for humans, sight is our most important sense. When a dog enters a new environment, it sniffs as it moves about. The sense of smell is his most important way of gathering information.

Dogs' sense of smell is far superior to ours – they can easily follow the route taken by a person or animal who passed by

Humans will look around when entering a new situation, whereas dogs will use their nose to find out what goes on there.

hours or days earlier, leaving no visible signs, and they can sniff out minute amounts of drugs or explosives through layers of packaging and containers. Their sense of smell is known to be at least 100 times more acute than ours and may be even better. The area inside a dog's nose that detects scent is about 14 times larger than ours and the nerves from this go to a part of the brain that is larger and further developed than the area of the human brain that processes information from the nose.

This amazing sense of smell allows dogs to detect odours that are lost to us completely. We should not be surprised that they spend hours investigating lamp posts where other dogs have left urine or when they put their noses in all the wrong places when investigating new people. They are doing as nature intended and gathering information. Being able to tell the age, sex, state of health, reproductive status and even state of mind from one sniff is a remarkable ability.

Knowing that dogs live in a world of scent rather than sight helps to explain why dogs sometimes do unusual things. For example, your dog may bark at you if he sees you approaching from a distance and only change this to a greeting response when you get within sniffing distance or if the wind blows your scent in his direction.

Dogs see shape, form and movement, whereas humans see detail and texture.

Sound sensitivity

Dogs are more sensitive to sounds than we are and can hear sounds that we cannot. This explains why they will sometimes appear to be listening intently when we can hear nothing – they can hear sounds from four times farther away than we can, so there is no need to shout when asking your dog to do something. Unless his hearing is impaired, your dog will easily hear what you are saying even if you are some distance away and if he is ignoring you it will have more to do with his motivation to listen and whether he is paying attention rather than his ability to hear.

Dogs of some breeds are likely to be more sensitive to sound than others. Those used for herding, such as collies and German shepherd dogs and their crosses, are likely to react to loud noises and are more prone to developing noise phobias than others.

They can also hear a high range of frequencies that allows them to hear ultrasonic sounds, such as mice squeaking. This explains a dog's ability to hear 'silent' dog whistles when we hear nothing and may help to explain why they get excited when they hear their owner's car approaching but will ignore others of the same make.

A physical feature that affects dogs' ability to hear is whether it has pricked ears or whether his ears hang down. Pricked ears will catch more sound and they are more mobile, which allows them to be rotated to pinpoint the source of the sound. A spaniel that runs in all directions to find his owner when called finds it hard to determine where the call came from because of his heavy ear flaps.

Selective sight

Dogs are not colour blind as used to be believed, but their colour vision is not as good as ours. This means that they will detect objects on a contrasting background better than if they blend in.

A dog is more likely to see a yellow ball on green grass, for example, than a red one. Dogs also see detail and texture less well and recognise objects by shape and form instead.

They are also much very sensitive to movement, especially movement at ground level, than we are as they evolved to catch moving animals. This makes it more likely that they will see a moving object, whether it is a rolling ball or a running cat, than a stationary one. They can also see at night and in dim conditions because they have a reflective layer at the back of their eyes. This traps light and allows them to make more use of it and is the reason a dog's eyes shine when caught in the beam of a car's headlights. The ability to see better at lower light levels helps wild dogs to hunt at dawn and dusk and allows domestic dogs to run off at top speed in darkness without crashing into things.

SEEING FROM A DIFFERENT PERSPECTIVE

A dog sees the world from a much lower perspective than we do. While this may seem obvious, it is often overlooked. This is why dogs jump up to greet their owners or to see out of windows. It becomes an important point when a dog is particularly small and has short legs. Thinking what it must be like for dogs to be in our giant world can help to explain some of their behaviour.

Jaws, paws and the sense of touch

Dogs use their mouths to hold or carry objects.

Another obvious difference between humans and dogs is that dogs do not have hands. Instead they use their mouths to pick up objects, to explore and for defence. Experienced dogs can be as accurate with their mouths as we are with our hands – if an adult dog bites and misses, it probably meant to!

It is also worth knowing that paws, neck and whisker areas around the sense organs can be particularly sensitive to touch. If dogs are being attacked, these are the areas they need to guard the most. A dog cannot run if one of his paws is injured; it is important to protect his vulnerable jugular vein in his neck when fighting; and the organs with which he senses the world are particularly vulnerable and important.

Appreciating these sensitivities can help to prevent you startling your dog by touching him on these areas unexpectedly or when he is asleep. You may notice that he jumps a little when

The dog in the middle of the picture above is not enjoying the attention and sits dowm and licks its nose to signal this to the others.

touched in these places so avoid these areas until he has learned to trust you. As your relationship with him develops, get him used to having his paws touched and held, and to being held around the neck. Many dogs are very sensitive around the head area, but they begin to tolerate and enjoy being touched there as they begin to relax and trust their humans.

Body language

Dogs usually communicate with each other using body language. This involves the use of the tail, ears, eyes, posture and facial expression to signal their intentions. They will automatically try to communicate with their owners using these signals too and if you can learn to read them you will be able to decipher what your dog is trying to tell you.

Learning body language is not difficult. The most important thing to do is to watch your dog in different situations. Look at his posture, at what his tail is doing, how he carries his ears, where he is looking and what he is doing with his mouth. Watch how he behaves and try to work out a reason for the action. You will soon be able to guess at how he is feeling just by looking at him if you watch him enough.

Why do dogs do that?

Having evolved from wolves, dogs are driven by similar needs to those that kept their ancestors alive. These are the need to live in a social group, the need to stay safe, the need to maintain their bodies and the need to reproduce.

All dogs are different, just as all people are different, and some will place different emphasis on certain behaviours and enjoy doing different things more than others. However, dogs are all basically the same and learning about their special species needs can help you to provide an outlet for their natural behaviour that will result in a contented, well behaved pet.

LEARNING BODY LANGUAGE

Hand signals
Dogs use vocal communication very little when 'talking' to each other and consequently find it difficult to learn words. They will learn hand signals much quicker because it taps into to their natural method of communication.

Tail wagging
A wagging tail is a sign of excitement, not just of happiness. A happy dog will wag his tail, but so will an excited dog that is about to bite. A stiff body posture and a wagging tail signals something very different from a body that is relaxed with a wagging tail.

Play bow
A play bow, with elbows on the floor and bottom in the air, is an invitation to play.

Head high
A confident dog holds his head high, his tail erect and looks directly at the source of interest. His ears are up and his mouth is relaxed.

Flattened body, tail down
A shy dog will flatten his body, keeping most of his weight on his back legs ready to run if necessary. The tail is often tucked under or held down. His ears are held back and his eyes are open wide so that the whites of his eyes can be seen. He will avoid looking at the person or animal that makes his feel shy but will glance in their direction and look away quickly.

All dogs need social contact, whether from humans or other dogs.

THE NEED FOR SOCIAL CONTACT

If wolves are to survive, it is important for them to live in a social group. This enables them to hunt, stay safe and reproduce. Pet dogs have retained this need for social contact, which is why they make such good pets. All dogs need to feel that they are part of a pack. This need can sometimes be overlooked if everyone in a household leads a busy life. Lack of attention and affection can become a problem if it persists as a dog will begin to behave badly just to get attention. Bad behaviour then becomes a nuisance and, sadly, it is often punished rather that treated as a symptom of an underlying need.

Lack of love and attention is unlikely to be a problem with a new dog. However, as the novelty begins to wear off and the family returns to normal routines, you need to reassure your dog that he is a valued member of your family. Try to set aside a quiet time each day to give your dog the undivided attention he needs. Play with him, stroke him, talk to him and let him know that he is important to you and the family. This should not be a chore, but it is often something that we need to consciously make time for with our busy lives.

Many of the behaviours displayed by dogs come from the need for social contact. Greeting rituals when you arrive home, face licking, pawing for attention or noses pushed under your hand, tail wagging and other gestures are all designed to keep us close and are done instinctively by the dog to promote the bond of friendship between us.

THE NEED TO STAY SAFE

All animals need to feel safe as the penalty for not being safe in the wild is death or injury. As it is so important, it takes priority over all other behaviour.

A new dog may take a long time to settle in, particularly if he was frightened in his previous home. He may feel very vulnerable at first and he may not want to play or even eat very much because he is on red alert all the time. In addition, he will be more likely to be defensive when approached or when his safety zone is breached. Growling, raising his lips or hackles, or hiding under tables or behind chairs will all be signs that he is not feeling safe. As he gains more confidence he may decide that the family is safe, but intruders are not and may show territorial behaviour designed to keep visitors away.

Some dogs are worse than others. Collies and German shepherd dogs and their crosses are particularly prone to being fearful and any dog that has had bad experiences or not enough socialisation as a puppy will take a long time to feel safe in a new environment. It takes time to build up the trust a dog needs to feel safe. Be a considerate owner who gives him the space he needs, but who works with him gently and gradually until he can overcome his fears to help him come round faster.

The desire to stay safe overrides all others. Getting away into a small space, which is easy to defend can help a dog feel less afraid.

Playing with toys is
domestic dogs' substitute for
hunting. It helps to keep
their bodies fit and active.

Some dogs are fine at home with the family, but are very scared of things they encounter when out for a walk. Things that move and make a noise, such as big lorries, children on bikes or skateboards, other animals or people can all frighten a dog that is unfamiliar with the world we live in. Take care not to overwhelm him with too much at first and keep your distance from these scary things to help him realise that these things will not hurt him.

Try not to expect a dog to lose his fears overnight. Fears are nature's way of keeping him safe and a dog will not lose the feeling of being afraid until he has had many positive experiences with whatever it was he is worried about. See Chapter 7 for more information.

Many other behaviours associated with staying safe may be displayed by a new dog. Tearing up items that smell of their owner, scratching at doors to get out of the house when left alone or marking the territory with urine to make themselves feel more secure are common behaviours in recently rehomed dogs. If your dog does something unusual during its first few days with you, it is likely that he is trying to make himself feel safer.

THE NEED TO MAINTAIN THEIR BODIES

A healthy body requires food and water and our dogs' ancestors had to travel to find both. This desire to exercise has been passed on to our domestic dogs. In addition, wolves have to hunt to eat and although most of our dogs no longer do this they have retained the motivation to behave in a similar way. Playing with toys is an acceptable substitute for hunting and fulfils the instinctive desire for dogs to chase and capture. It can also help to ensure that your dog is so busy concentrating on you that he is not getting into trouble chasing other things that move, such

Chewing is necessary for healthy teeth and jaws. Dogs like to do this throughout their lives not just as puppies.

DIFFERENT GAMES

● Chase games: the most popular game played particularly by herding breeds. Most dogs love the thrill of the chase and the desire to stop the 'prey' from moving is strong.
● Possession games: it is important for dogs to keep hold of items in their possession. Once these would have been pieces of meat or hide, but we can substitute pieces of rubber or rope.
● Squeaky toy games: these stimulate a very primitive instinct to bite and 'kill' a squeaking object. Terriers, bred to catch and kill small animals, usually enjoy this game. How excited a dog gets when it plays this game will give you an indication of how strong its predatory instinct is.

DOGS THAT WON'T PLAY

If your dog will not play with toys, it might be because he has not learned to do so or has played too much with another dog rather than humans. Begin with soft toys, particularly those covered in fake fur, to stimulate his instincts. Keep it moving quickly and erratically, concentrating on the toy rather than your dog. Have fun yourself throwing it to a partner or throwing it in the air until he begins to want to join in the game. Allow him to catch it and end the game while he is still wanting more. He will gradually begin to have more fun playing with you and the toy and you will be able to play for longer.

as cats, sheep, wild animals, cars or children on bikes.

Domestic dogs also display other behaviours associated with body maintenance. They will often clean themselves by licking and self grooming, they may bury excess food to keep it safe for later or dig out to a cool or warm place to lie. Chewing to maintain the teeth and jaws is something that dogs like to do throughout their life. As commercial pet food is often not chewy, provide suitable items that they can chew on to fulfil this desire.

THE NEED TO REPRODUCE

Animals have evolved a desire to pass on their genes to the next generation. An entire dog will instinctively try to mate with receptive members of the opposite sex. Male dogs will take any opportunity to mate, particularly when there is a bitch in season nearby, whereas bitches have a 'season' or 'heat' period about twice a year.

Dogs do vary, however, in the effort they are willing to make to achieve their goal. Some entire dogs will happily remain at home if there is a bitch in season down the road, while others will escape and camp outside until the season is over. Similarly, bitches will differ in their desire to escape during seasons. Male dogs that have a strong desire to mate may show other unwanted behaviours such as escaping and roaming, and mounting cushions, blankets, peoples legs and small children. If you own a male dog that does this have him castrated to take away the urge and the unwanted behaviour. This is ultimately kinder to him than keeping him in a frustrated state or punishing the unwanted behaviour as it occurs. Similarly, spaying bitches will prevent them from escaping at the critical time in their season and presenting you with a litter of unwanted puppies a couple of months later.

What happens when you frustrate canine needs

Ignore these basic needs at your peril! Frustrating a dog's desire to maintain social contact with his group, stay safe, run, jump, play and chew will usually have unpleasant consequences as he tries to find fulfilment anyway.

A dog denied social contact will persistently seek attention or will try to escape to find social groups elsewhere. A dog that feels unsafe will show a range of unwanted defensive behaviours. A

dog denied the opportunity to exercise fully is likely to move about constantly and get in your way or will look for things to do that you may not approve of. Outside, he is likely to run off and not return and, if he is not playing appropriate games with toys, he will be playing inappropriate games with other things that move. A dog denied the chance to chew appropriate items will select your best shoes or anything accidentally dropped on the floor instead.

Knowing your dog's special species needs and giving him an outlet for them all will create a dog that is content and well behaved. Suppressing his basic needs or ignoring them will create a frustrated dog and bad behaviour.

Playing with toys out on a walk can help to keep your dog interested in you. He is then less likely to wander off and get into trouble.

BUILDING A FRIENDSHIP

There is nothing as effective as playing with toys to develop the bond between you and your new dog. Playing exposes strengths and weaknesses and allows you to get to know each other better. It is important to play a lot with your new dog, teaching him to do so first if necessary.

CHAPTER

6

Essential Training

Teaching your dog to come back when called, walk well on the lead and sit and lie down when told makes life easier, safer and more pleasant for you both. He may know some of the commands already and it would be wise to test out a variety of words and hand signals to check. Unfortunately, many dogs know the word 'sit' and little else, but if you use positive methods, training should be fun and rewarding.

A well trained dog makes everyday tasks easier and more pleasant.

Progression towards good manners and behaviour should begin as soon as you get your dog home, but training him to respond to commands can be left until a good relationship has developed between you. He will be more willing to please you if you are established as the leader of his social group and a friend, and this will take time to develop.

POINTS TO REMEMBER WHEN TRAINING

- Keep lessons short. Ten three-minute sessions are much better than one 30-minute session.
- Always end on a good note. Ask for something you know your dog can do and reward him well.
- Stop immediately if you feel yourself becoming frustrated or angry.
- Reward the correct action immediately.

Hand signals are easier than words

A dog will find it much easier to read your body language than listen to the words you speak. You can help your dog to learn words by giving hand, arm or body signals at the same time as you say the command. Once he responds every time, you can gradually reduce the body signals until just the spoken word remains.

Dogs can't be trained in a day

It will take a couple of months of regular teaching and many, many repetitions before what you are teaching will become permanently fixed in your dog's mind. Try not to expect too much of him too soon, particularly if you want him to respond to spoken words only.

Although he is a sophisticated and complex animal, he is not designed to learn to respond to spoken words and it is quite hard for him to learn them. If in doubt, always assume he has not quite understood it yet and show him what to do.

Different circumstances, different places

Remember that all dogs learn a set of associations surrounding an event. In order for your dog to learn that the word you say equals an action he performs, which equals a reward given to him by you, you will have to repeat the teaching process in many different locations under altered circumstances. Eventually, your dog will realise that all the associations surrounding the action other than the word itself are irrelevant and that you will give the reward whenever he does the required action when he hears the word wherever he is.

Distractions

Dogs learn better if they are taught in a quiet, calm environment with no distractions. However, once your dog has learned what you require, you will need to slowly increase the level of distraction and teach your dog that he has to respond to your requests even if he would prefer to do something else. This will require you to keep him controlled at first so that he cannot run off to be 'rewarded' by the distraction instead. Continue to build up the distractions until he will work for you even when he has very powerful urges to do something else.

Close control

Until you can more or less guarantee that your dog will respond to your requests; keep him under physical control so that he cannot be rewarded by running off and doing what he wants to do.

Above: Take titbits and toys out with you so that you can incorporate short training sessions throughout your walks.

Kind and effective ways to train

Dogs learn more quickly and remember more if they are rewarded for doing the right thing rather than punished for doing something wrong. The most effective training involves rewards and incentives and is fun and enjoyable for both parties.

Find out what motivates your dog. What does he like to do most – eat, chase balls, tug on toys, kill squeaky toys, be stroked, be praised? If he likes to do one or all of these things you can use them as an incentive and reward for responding to your requests. If, instead, he prefers to run free or hunt, life will be more difficult for you because you will need to teach him to enjoy playing and interacting with you first. This will take time and it should be done before you start any training. There is nothing more frustrating than trying to teach a dog that has no interest in you or your incentives. If you are not succeeding in getting him to play with toys, try feeding him by hand for a week so that he learns that you are a source of what he needs to survive. Once he is focusing on the food, begin to put some inside toys so that he starts to see these as a source of interest too.

Rewards can be made more enticing by withholding them for a period before training. Who wants another chocolate biscuit when you have just eaten a whole packet? This is difficult to do with affection and is a good reason why pet dogs need other incentives to encourage them to make the extra effort to learn what you want them to do.

COMING BACK WHEN CALLED

Being able to call your dog back to you ensures that he can be let off the lead safely and it is one of the most important things to teach your dog.

STEP 1

STEP 1: Begin in the house and garden. Call your dog enthusiastically and make sure you have a good reward ready for him when he reaches you. Gradually build this up, practising frequently throughout the day and rewarding well each time, until he is rushing to you at top speed whenever you call, even if he is busy doing something else.

STEP 2   STEP 3

Step 2: Take your dog, on a long lead or piece of line, to a quiet area and wait until he has explored his surroundings. When he is looking away from you, but is not too engrossed in something else, call him enthusiastically using the same words and tone you did at home and reward him well if he comes to you. If he does not, tug the lead praising him well when he moves a few paces towards you. Run backwards and enthusiastically encourage him to move with you. Reward him well when he gets to you.

Step 3: If your dog enjoys chase games, make a toy obvious to him then throw it behind you to encourage him to run up right up to you next time. Don't throw it too far or he will pull you over as he runs to get it.

Step 4: Once he has the toy, use the lead to bring him back to you and let him know how pleased you are. Praise him while he is holding the toy for a few moments first and then take it from him. Do not touch the toy or the area around his head for a while or he will begin to avoid coming back in case you take the toy.

STEP 4

Practice makes perfect

Step 5: When he responds readily to your call, practise when your dog is engrossed in something else. Use the lead to pull him away from whatever he is doing and enforce your command if necessary. Doing this will begin to make him more reliable about coming when called even when he would rather be doing something else. Once he has come back to you, let him go back to what he was doing to reward him.

Step 6: Continue to practise regularly until he responds every time despite any distractions going on around him. Use a washing line or similar long line as a lead to increase the amount of freedom he has and continue to practise in different areas until he is reliable. When you have this mental control, find a quiet area away from traffic, other dogs or livestock and let him off the lead (but make sure he is wearing a collar and identity disc just in case he runs off). Allow him freedom for a while before practising your recall. Reward him well and let him run free again.

STEP 5

STEP 6

WALKING ON A LOOSE LEAD

If your dog walks nicely on the lead, family members will be more willing to take him out for walks. He will be better exercised and, consequently, better behaved. There are two ways to achieve this: one is to fit a specially designed head collars and the other is to teach him not to pull when on the lead.

Wearing a headcollar

If you do decide to use a headcollar, follow the fitting instructions carefully and ignore your dog's attempts to scratch it off. Some dogs will seems quite frantic at first, but they will soon overcome their worries if you persevere. Most dogs learn to tolerate these devices very well and they are an ideal way to prevent pulling. Remember, though, not to tug or pull the lead sharply as this can damage your dog's neck. Once your dog has got used to the feel of something fitted around his nose and behind his ears, you can use it to control the position of his head so that he cannot pull.

TEACHING YOUR DOG NOT TO PULL

Dogs learn quickly and will soon realise they cannot pull when wearing a headcollar.

Most dogs pull on the lead because they want to go faster. If your dog learns that each time he pulls you stop, he will eventually walk without pulling. This method works well for all dogs, but takes considerable perseverance, particularly for dogs that have

been pulling their owners around for years. Practise at first in a quiet area when you do not need to get anywhere in a hurry. You can speed up the process by tiring your dog before you begin. Throw a toy for him in the garden until he tires or allow him to let off steam by giving him access to an open area before attempting to train him.

The key is to be persistent. Never allow the lead to go tight without stopping. If you have to be somewhere in a hurry, use a head collar so you do not set back your training. Begin training as soon as you put the lead on and do not allowing your dog to pull you as you leave the house. The first few walks may take a long time, but it will get easier and quicker as he learns.

STEP 1

STEP 2

STEP 3

STEP 1: If the lead begins to tighten, stop and stand still. For very boisterous dogs or persistent pullers, use your weight to bring them to an abrupt halt with a tug on the collar.

STEP 2: Keep your hands quite close to your body to give you maximum stability as your dog pulls. As he turns to find out why you have stopped, encourage him to come back to you. If he continues to pull away from you, give little tugs on the lead so that he cannot lean on it and encourage him to come back to you when he stops pulling.

STEP 3: TRY TO encourage him to return to his position beside you.

STEP 4: As soon as he is in position, praise him well and begin to walk forward at a fast pace. Praise him and continue to walk forward for as long as the lead remains loose.

STEP 5: Walking without pulling does not mean your dog must stay close to you all the time. With a long lead, or a flexi-lead, your dog can have quite a lot of freedom. However, as soon as the lead goes tight, begin again from Step 1 and repeat the exercise as frequently as necessary.

STEP 4

STEP 5

'SIT', 'DOWN' AND 'STAY'

These are three useful words for your dog to know and they are easy to teach. He may know them already, but could need a refresher course to sharpen his responses.

STEP 1

STEP 2

STEP 3

'Sit'

STEP 1: Offer a reward and ask your dog to sit. If he does not, hold a tasty titbit in front of his nose.

STEP 2: Move the titbit up and backwards. As his nose follows it, his bottom should go down. If your dog moves backwards instead, position him in the corner of the room so that he is unable to do so.

STEP 3: Feed the titbit as soon as your dog's bottom touches the floor and praise him well while he remains sitting.

Continue with this sequence over several sessions until your dog begins to understand what he is expected to do. Eventually you will find that he will begin to learn what is expected and will sit when you hold the titbit above him. Practise in different locations and circumstances until he sits reliably when you ask.

STEP 1

STEP 2

'Down'

STEP 1: Ensure your dog is in the sitting position. Offer something that he wants and move it down towards the floor. It is usually easier if you offer a titbit instead of a toy as you can hide food in your hand and your dog cannot get it until you release it.

STEP 2: Keep his attention on whatever it is, but do not allow him to take it. Eventually, he will become tired of holding his head down and will begin to lie down to get more comfortable.

STEP 3: As soon as he lies down, give him the reward and praise him well.

STEP 3

STEP 1

STEP 2

'Stay'

STEP 1: Ensure your dog is sitting. Ask him to stay and stand still beside him. Wait for a short time then praise him gently for remaining in position. If he gets up at any time, replace him in the position in exactly the same spot and repeat. If he gets up repeatedly, you may need to exercise him more before the next training session or spend more time teaching him how to sit or lie down on request.

STEP 2: Once he has learned to stay still when you are beside him, ask him to stay and take a step to the side. Use the lead to stop him from getting up if you can and put him in the same place if he moves. Wait a short time and then move back to him and praise him gently while in position as before. Progress until you no longer need to keep him on the lead.

STEP 3: When he is happy to stay while you move to the side, progress to moving in front of him. A hand signal will help him to understand what you mean and can be used to supplement the word if he looks as though he may move. Move back to him and praise him gently as before.

Gradually build up this exercise until your dog will stay still for longer periods and in different positions. These exercises are

STEP 3

TIP

Never ask your dog to stay without tethering him when you leave him unattended in public places. There are many distractions that may cause him to move, which could result in a nasty incident.

useful for times when you want him to stay in the car when you open the door until you have attached a lead, for example, or you want him to settle down and lie still beside you while you visit a friend. The word 'stay' can then be used to help him to understand what he is supposed to do in these situations.

DOG TRAINING CLASSES

Training classes can help you solve training problems and bolster your enthusiasm for training until your dog has reached a suitable standard. However, many rescue dogs are afraid of other dogs or people and being in a crowded hall full of both may push him into behaving aggressively. If your dog is shy or already aggressive with people or dogs, it may be better to train him at home or arrange individual tuition first.

If you do decide to attend dog training classes, go along without your dog first to see if you approve of their methods. The trainer should use rewards rather than punishment: toys and titbits should be used rather than choke chains. Ask your veterinary surgeon for a recommendation or contact the Association of Pet Dog Trainers, which monitors the methods used by its members and ensures they are kind, fair and effective.

CHAPTER

7

Coping with Shyness and Aggression

If you have chosen your dog carefully using the methods suggested earlier, you are unlikely to see real aggression from your dog unless you have been unlucky or have deliberately taken on a problem dog as a challenge. However, as dogs cannot talk to us and tell us what is wrong and if we ignore their body language, as we so frequently do, they have only one way of telling us to stop what we are doing. While most dogs settle into their new homes without problems, it helps to know some of the causes of aggression so you can heed any warning signs.

Reasons for aggression

Dogs do not become aggressive without reason. Most aggressive incidents happen because the dog is afraid and is acting defensively. Sometimes he may be guarding resources, such as food or the territory, which he thinks he needs to protect. Or he may be trying to raise his status within the pack. Some dogs will be aggressive to other smaller animals because their predatory instincts are triggered. If your dog is being aggressive, seek professional help from a pet behaviour counsellor (see Chapter 9).

FEAR AND SHYNESS

Most fears arise from a lack of socialisation with people and other animals when the dog was a puppy. Unsocialised dogs are also unfamiliar with many things in their environment, which adds to their fears. Dogs that have this problem are usually shy and fearful when taken to new places. They are often suspicious of new people, especially those in dark clothes or wearing or carrying anything unusual. Men are often mistrusted more than women as puppies are often raised by women and may have limited contact with men in their early weeks.

An unpleasant experience, whether frightening or painful, can ensure that the dog becomes fearful when the same circumstances occur again and bad treatment from owners or others can result in fears of certain types of people. Mother dogs who are fearful themselves can pass on their fears to their puppies.

A frightened dog will often appear crouched, ready to run and may pant rapidly.

WARNING SIGNS

If your dog is upset with you, he will usually try to let you know before he takes the drastic action of biting. These are the warning signs:

- He will use obvious body language, such as slight crouching, flattened ears and lowered tail, and will look intently at you.
- If this is ignored he will growl and raise his lips to show his teeth.
- He may stiffen and stare.
- Often he will snap in the air, close to your skin, to show you that he means business.

Ignoring any of these signals is not wise as it may result in a real bite. Punishing these behaviours is also counterproductive as the dog will learn not to give warnings before it bites, which results in an unpredictable dog. This may have happened to your dog in the past and you may find that a slight change in his body language is all that precedes a bite.

It is essential that you avoid situations where your dog may become aggressive. If, however, he exhibits any of these warning signs, defuse the situation by stopping what you are doing immediately (see page 108).

A dog showing defensive
aggression does not look
frightened even though he
is. This dog is putting up a
good display to make
the recipient back down.

Four defence strategies

If an animal feels under threat, it can adopt one of four strategies for dealing with the threat and can switch between them rapidly and without warning. These strategies are fight, flight, freeze and appease.

Fight: dogs may make lots of noise and frightening visual displays to try to prevent a threat from coming closer. When this fails, or if a threat is approaching too fast, it can choose to fight and bite to make a threat retreat. Dogs will often use biting only as a last resort as the penalties of being injured in any retaliation are usually seen as too high. However, once a dog is forced to use this strategy, it will quickly discover how effective it is and is more likely to use it again. In order to use this strategy, a dog needs a certain amount of self-confidence. Confident dogs, especially those on home ground, near other members of their pack and in small, easily defendable spaces are more likely to choose this strategy than dogs on their own in a strange place.

Flight: running away is the safest form of defence if a dog has somewhere to run to and if he is not fastened to his owner or a fixed point by a lead. The 'flight' option is not as effective for a dog in a small territory, such as a car, cage or small fenced garden, and so it will often choose the 'fight' option instead.

Freeze: keeping still and hoping the threat will go away is a strategy that sometimes works. However, dogs in the freeze position will be ready to adopt one of the other strategies if this one fails. Gentle, shy dogs are likely to adopt this strategy.

Appease: when faced with another animal, which appears higher in rank or dangerous, puppies or young dogs will often show appeasement gestures. They may lick their muzzles, flatten their ears, raise a paw, roll over, lift a hind leg to expose the groin area, produce a small amount of urine or some or all of these. These gestures are designed to show the stronger animal that they are no threat and, hence, that there is no need to use aggression. Some dogs carry this strategy into adulthood, but most reserve it for members of their own pack as they mature.

Physiological changes

When an animal is under threat hormones and other chemicals are released into the blood stream, the heart rate and breathing get faster and the blood supply to vital organs increases. A dog under threat may tremble or shake, pant in short rapid breaths, sweat through his pads and will probably want to go to the toilet soon after it detects a threat.

TIP

Be jolly rather than sympathetic if your dog is scared. If he sees that you are not worried, he will be more likely to forget his own fears.

Tasty titbits offered by a stranger can help shy dogs to overcome their fear.

These bodily changes will subside quite quickly after the initial fright, but the physiological changes persist for some days afterwards so that if the threat returns, the dog is prepared. Remember this if your dog is shy or fearful. An experience that upsets him, such as being taken to a new home or being treated by the veterinary surgeon, can be enough to activate these changes. For some days after a fright, and possibly during the early days of his new life in your family, your dog may be more easily triggered into defensive behaviour than normal.

Coping with shyness

Many dogs are shy and afraid of the unfamiliar. If your dog is like this when you get him, he may take a while to settle down. If you keep him relatively calm and expose him to new situations slowly, never going beyond what he can cope with, he should begin to get braver. However, if you take things too fast, particularly if you force him to have encounters with things that scare him, he is likely to get worse and may even begin to be aggressive in his own defence.

In order not to overwhelm a shy dog, watch his body language and learn to tell when he is enjoying an experience and when he is becoming afraid (see page 81). Watch his ear and tail carriage particularly as these will give you the first clues. Identify what scares him most – is it strangers, other dogs or new environments? Once you know the cause, give him a controlled exposure to small amounts of whatever it is that scares him.

Combine this with activities that he enjoys, such as playing or eating, and he will become more confident more quickly. If your dog is frightened of traffic, for example, take him to where he can see traffic in the distance, but is not afraid. Play with him and make it fun to be in that place and then move a little closer to the traffic. Continue until you think your dog is on the edge of what he can cope with. End on a positive note and finish for the day. If you do this every day, keeping away from close encounters with traffic until he is cured, he will soon realise that it will not hurt him. It will take some time to overcome the problem completely, as with all fears, but you should begin to see results quite quickly.

It is important that owners of shy dogs take charge to ensure that their dog feels safe at all times. Once your dog begins to trust that you will be there to help him out of difficulties, he will relax and enjoy himself.

This dog is worried and is moving away so that he feels safer. Forcing him to confront his fear by pulling him closer could result in him using aggression instead.

Aggression to strangers

Nearly all aggression to strangers is caused by fear. Even common territorial aggression to postmen and other visitors is caused by a mistrust of people coming onto the property. If your dog has bitten anyone, it is up to you to ensure it never happens again. It is essential to keep complete control of your dog at all times and it is important to get professional help to identify the cause of the problem and to work our a treatment programme.

Tackling the problem alone can be frightening and fraught with difficulties so ask your veterinary surgeon to refer you to a member of the Association of Pet Behaviour Counsellors (see page 158). You can also ask the rescue centre that rehomed your dog for help.

If your dog is likely to snap, accustom him to wearing a muzzle. Although they look cumbersome, basket muzzles are less restricting than the tube style and allow more circulation of air around the tongue.

INTRODUCING YOUR DOG TO A MUZZLE

If your dog is likely to be aggressive, buy a well fitting muzzle and get him used to wearing it. To do this, put the muzzle on him a few minutes before something nice is going to happen to him, such as dinner time, someone arriving home or a game with a toy. Ignore any of his attempts to remove the muzzle and praise him when he accepts it. During one of the acceptance periods, remove the muzzle and immediately reward him. After a few days he will begin to accept the muzzle and you will be able to leave it on for longer. If you do this, your dog will associate the muzzle with pleasant things about to happen, and you will have no trouble in getting it on him in future. If he associates it only with unpleasant things, such as a trip to the veterinary surgery, he will be very intolerant of it.

Make sure he is wearing the muzzle whenever there is a chance that he may be aggressive. Muzzles are restricting and do tend to make fear-biters more fearful, but they do at least prevent a bite. If you have a large dog you are not sure of, it is safer to muzzle him when he goes to the veterinary surgeon, at least for the first few times, just in case. Even the most docile dog can become aggressive in defence if he is in pain so accustoming your dog to a muzzle may be a wise precaution.

FEAR OF STRANGERS

If your dog barks at people or shows signs that he may be frightened, it is possible to change his attitude to strangers. To do this, arrange for your dog to meet strangers one at a time in a calm atmosphere so he can get used to them gradually.

Begin by putting your dog into a back room when a visitor arrives so he does not meet them on the doorstep where his excitement levels will be greatest. Ask the visitor to sit down and arm them with toys and titbits if they are willing to help. When all is settled, bring your dog in on a lead and sit away from the visitor. Wait until your dog has settled down before asking the visitor to encourage him to come forward to receive titbits and, perhaps, a game with a toy. If there is any doubt about your dog, prevent him from going too close and ask your visitor to throw the titbits or toys. Ask your visitor not to stare at your dog or make sudden movements that may scare him. End on a positive note and take your dog out of the room before your visitor gets up to leave.

Introductions made in this way will teach your dog to look forward to the arrival of that particular person, but they may have

Yawning can be one of the first signs that your dog is uneasy about his situation.

to visit several times before your dog goes forward to greet them. Keep the visitor sitting down at first and gradually work up to them getting up and moving around as your dog begins to accept them. You can speed up this process by arranging to meet on neutral territory and trying to get some gentle interaction going between the two of them, such as a game.

When your dog has got to know one person, try again with another. It may be a good idea to start with women as they are usually better accepted by shy dogs, and work up to introducing men. Increasing your dog's circle of friends in this way will build his confidence in people and he will begin to see them as a source of interest and fun rather than being afraid.

Throughout the process, ensure that your dog approaches each visitor first rather than the other way around. Try to keep to one visitor at a time until he can cope with more. Never punish or scold unwanted behaviour, but distract him instead by, for example, asking him to come to you and sit, and praising him. Try to relax and make sure you are in control of the situation so that your dog is not overwhelmed at any stage. If you have a number of people visiting at any time or anyone who is frightened of dogs, it may be best to keep him shut in another room until they have gone.

FEAR OF CHILDREN

If your dog is aggressive towards children, you sould seek professional help from a pet behaviour counsellor and keep him under control and muzzled until he has changed his attitude towards them.

If your dog is worried about children, take great care to ensure that they do not crowd him or get too close, which may make him feel threatened. Watch carefully when children are around and move him to a safe place if you see that he is becoming worried. Always insist that your dog approaches the children rather than the other way around and if he does not want to go to them, don't force him. Try to get him playing with the children in the garden and give them tasty titbits to throw to him. This will help to change his attitude towards them, but ensure they do not accidentally go near him and scare him until he has begun to see them as friends.

Many dogs are unfamiliar with toddlers and smaller children and find it difficult to cope with them because they squeal, move erratically and can pinch and pull fur when up close. If you have very young children or they visit you, it may be best to use a stair gate so that your dog is not isolated, but is kept out of the room that the children are in.

Aggression to owners

When your dog first comes home he will not know the people in the household and may not trust them at first. He may be particularly mistrustful if he has been punished or mistreated by previous owners. In addition, the stress of all the changes will make him more reactive and defensive. Any growls or warnings that happen in the first few days should be accepted as part of the settling in process. Try not to retaliate or be disappointed by your new dog, but try to avoid the same situation happening again. Make an extra effort to win your dog's trust and affection.

COLLAR SHYNESS

Many dogs are wary of being held by the collar and may bite if grabbed suddenly. A dog's neck is a sensitive area and it is where dogs will bite each other when they begin fighting. In addition, many dogs have learned that when they are held by the collar, there is no escape. They may have been grabbed in the past and held while they were punished or dragged somewhere they were afraid of going.

If your dog has a tendency to be worried when held by the collar, get him used to being held by approaching slowly and in a friendly way. Talk to him and try to let him know that your intentions are good. You may need to get him to come to you at first, rather than you approaching him. Hold his collar, feed him a tasty treat and release him. Continue to do this on a regular basis, gradually increasing the speed with which you approach him until he begins to trust you.

PAIN-RELATED AGGRESSION

If your dog is in pain, he may not trust you enough to let you help, particularly if he is new to the family. If your dog has an accident or needs to be given treatment, such as ear drops in a sore ear, it may take a while before you both trust each other enough to do it easily.

Take things slowly and muzzle him if necessary. If necessary, put the muzzle on a few minutes in advance of any treatment so he does not associate the two procedures and begin to resent being muzzled. Do not get cross with him or punish him for showing aggression as this will aggravate the problem. Try not to be disappointed that he is acting in this way. You cannot tell him that you are doing what is best for him – trust is something that comes only with time.

REDIRECTED AGGRESSION

Dogs sometimes bite humans without meaning to when they are in a frenzy about something else. If you try to break up a fight between two dogs, for example, your dog may bite by accident. Similarly, if your dog has seen another dog that it would like to be aggressive to and you are restraining it, he may turn and bite without really thinking he is biting you. It is therefore best to keep away from dogs that are highly aroused and use a lead or other means, such as a cushion, to take them away from the situation to calm down.

DOMINANCE AGGRESSION TO OWNERS

Some dogs are ambitious and want to lead the pack. If you chose your dog well and put in place all the suggestions in Chapter 4 as soon as you got your dog home, he should realise that his place is below all the humans in the household. However, as his confidence gradually increases, he may begin to get more pushy with whoever he perceives as being the weakest member of the household. If he begins to get aggressive, seek professional help from a pet behaviour counsellor. If he is just starting to get pushy, enforce all the rules in Chapter 4 rigorously and ensure that you and all in your family win all encounters with him for the next few months.

Aggression to other dogs

Some dogs are aggressive when on the lead, but are all right if they are loose because they know that they are able to run away if necessary. If your dog is aggressive to others, it is important that you take control of him and keep other dogs safe. Even if he does not hurt other dogs, he can scare them, which can in turn cause other dogs to become afraid and aggressive with others. You are also likely to get into trouble with other owners if you do not keep your dog under control. Get professional help from a pet behaviour counsellor if your dog is seriously aggressive.

The dog on the left has chosen the 'fight' option in an effort to scare away the other dog, which has come too close for comfort.

DEFENSIVE AGGRESSION

As with aggression towards humans, most aggression towards other dogs is caused by fear. This may be due to a lack of socialisation with other dogs at an early age or it could be caused by an unpleasant experience in the dog's past.

Dogs often do not have enough confidence to use aggression as a way of coping with the fear they feel when they are new to an area so you may begin to see a change in your dog after the first few weeks. The best way to deal with any displays of aggression towards other dogs is to focus his attention on you.

Practise at first in an area where you can put a distance between you both and other dogs. Take out his favourite toys and treats, stand still and let him explore. When he begins to look at the other dogs, call him to you and play enthusiastically or offer tasty treats. Move steadily closer to the other dogs, repeating this procedure each time he looks at them. Gradually, after several sessions, you will find that he begins to look towards you whenever he sees another dog. Reward him well when he does.

If he will not play or eat, or if he begins to get agitated, you may be too close to the other dogs. Move farther away and try again. If your dog will not play or eat when out on a walk, even in the absence of other dogs, you will need to teach him to do this first (see below).

Avoid close encounters with other dogs if possible until he is feeling more confident as bad experiences will set back your progress. If, however, you can't avoid other dogs, cross the road if you see one approaching, put your body between your dog and the other one, ask your dog to sit and try to keep him focused on the reward. Keep working with him until the other dog passes, reward him well and continue with your walk.

He will gradually learn that you become a source of interesting, pleasant things when other dogs are about and will prefer to concentrate on these rather than deal with the fear he feels when concentrating on the other dog. He will learn that you keep him safe and out of trouble and that when, he is with you, he has no need to try to keep other dogs away by using aggressive behaviour. This takes time and perseverance, as with the treatment of all fear-based problems, but you should see improvements gradually. If you do not progress, seek advice from a pet behaviour counsellor.

One of the worst things you can do for dogs that are afraid of other dogs is to take them to a conventional dog training class. Here they will be in close contact with many of the creatures they fear the most and it will make them worse rather than better.

FRUSTRATED PLAY

Some dogs enjoy playing with other dogs so much that they can become very frustrated when prevented from doing so by their lead. These dogs will have grown up playing with other dogs instead of playing with humans and will consider it a very important part of their life. For the more boisterous and determined, this frustration can develop into aggression that may appear to be directed towards other dogs. When allowed off the lead, they will often play nicely, if sometimes roughly, with others.

Such a dog will need to be taught that he cannot play with all the dogs he meets and that you will select those he can play with. Withdrawing all opportunity to play at first is likely to make him slightly worse, so he should have regular access to another playful dog if possible. After this, take him out and teach him how you want him to behave in the presence of other dogs. Teaching a dog how to play with people is difficult, but can be very rewarding as he will then begin to focus on you when outside rather than trying to get to every other dog he sees. You will need to be as determined about this as he is about trying to play with other dogs, but you will begin to see results and his behaviour should improve in time.

Predatory aggression

Predatory instincts are present to a greater degree in some dogs than others. Terriers and lurchers tend to have strong instincts for catching and killing, but not all dogs will be like this and some other breeds may also have these tendencies. Predatory aggression is likely to be directed at anything that is small, that squeaks or cries and moves quickly or erratically. Anything appearing injured or weak is more likely to be targeted.

Owners often find it difficult to believe that the dog they cuddle and that appears so loving is capable of killing, but they forget that dogs do not have our sense of what is right and wrong. A dog that shows this type of aggression is no more prone to other forms of aggression. There is no need to worry that, as a result of catching and killing next door's rabbit, he is likely to try to sneak up the stairs and grab you by the throat in the night. Dogs with a strong predatory drive are only dangerous to animals that look and behave like prey animals. This does, sometimes, include new born babies, but attacks on babies are, thankfully, very rare.

If your dog has a predatory nature, there is little that you can do other than be very aware of the problem and prevent contact with vulnerable creatures. Be careful never to leave him alone anywhere he can get to small pets' cages. Predatory behaviour can be inhibited in some dogs with firm handling, but it is safer to keep them away from trouble altogether.

Dogs that chase live-stock are usually more interested in the 'thrill of the chase' than in predation.

CHAPTER

8

Alone at Home

Some dogs will find it difficult to cope with being left alone in their new house at first. For some, the rehoming experience may have been quite traumatic and they will need time to settle down. Others may have had separation problems in a previous home or may have never have been left alone at all before.

Many dogs wait patiently for their owners to return, but some become very distressed when separated from their pack.

Whatever the reason, dogs that are destructive, make a noise or are dirty in the house can be difficult to live with. It is important that a speedy resolution is found to the problem. It is encouraging to know that most dogs gradually improve as time goes on, but it is also worth knowing that there are things you can do to speed up the process. You first need to find out why your dog is behaving in this way.

Punishment does not work

Never punish your dog when you return home regardless of what he has done. Punishment after the event will not prevent it happening again. If the problem was caused by anxiety, punishment will probably make it worse. Sadly, owners often punish their dogs, partly because they are angry that their belongings have been ruined and partly because they think their dog looks 'guilty'. What the dog is actually doing is showing submission in response to their anger. Dogs are very sensitive to our moods and body language, and your dog will notice immediately if you are not pleased by what you have discovered upon opening the door. A natural display of submission to this posture is often seen by us as guilt and evidence that 'he knows he has done something wrong'.

The truth is that your dog does not know his behaviour was wrong since no one stopped him at the time. He was just acting in a manner appropriate to his motivations. Punishing him when you return will not work because he will not understand what you are punishing him for. He can remember what he did, but you have no way of linking the action with the punishment, even if you take him to the scene of the crime. The intelligent way forward is to put him in another room while you clear up the mess or until you are ready to greet him in a friendly way and then think about what you can do to make him feel more comfortable about being left alone next time.

Will another dog help?

Getting another dog to solve a separation problem will probably mean that you will end up with two dogs with the same problem. This is particularly true for anxiety or fear-based problems as these are very easily passed on to another dog. Unfortunately, in most cases a second dog is no substitute for a human and so the 'problem' dog continues to have the problem.

It is natural for dogs to want to be with their pack leader. Rescue dogs need time to learn that you have not abandoned them and that you will return.

A second dog will really help only in cases where the 'problem' dog has been used to living with another dog and now finds itself on its own. If you are lucky, and the second dog proves to be a suitable substitute for the dog that is missing, the problem may well subside.

Leaving calmly and without a big fuss can help your dog remain at ease.

Establish a good departure routine

It is important to start as you mean to go on and this is especially true when it comes to leaving your dog alone. Some owners will take a week or two off when they first get their new dog to help him settle in. However, they usually find that on their first day back to work their dog has been unable to cope with the sudden isolation and they return to a chewed or messy house or complaining neighbours.

From day one, it is important for your new dog to learn that he cannot be with you all the time. Begin by leaving him in the room where you intend him to sleep several times for a short period on his first day while you are elsewhere in the house. Leave him alone in the house on the second day for several short periods if possible. This will mean that if you go out to work your dog will be better able to tolerate your absence because it has been part of what he has become used to. Some dogs will take longer to settle than this and, if you find your new dog will not tolerate being isolated from you without panicking, you may need to take things more slowly.

TIP

Leave a tape or video recorder running to help you discover what your dog does when you leave and to help you to identify the exact nature and cause of his problem.

Over-attachment to new owners

Being taken from a home where everything is familiar, left in kennels for a period of time and then finding yourself in a different home where everything is new and strange can be a very unsettling experience. Upon finding themselves in a new home, many dogs want to stick like glue to their new owner and find it very difficult to cope when they are left behind at first.

Dogs most likely to become over-attached are those that feel vulnerable for some reason and those with very little self-confidence. Very young and very old dogs may feel vulnerable, dogs that have been abused or punished a lot may lack confidence and those with gentle, submissive natures who would not want to use the fight option as a means of defence are often worried when left.

Many dogs come in to rescue centres when they reach adolescence. This is a time when dogs would be dispersing from the nest in the wild and becoming more independent. In a pet home, dogs will go through this process with owners, gradually becoming less dependent as they mature. However, if you enforce the separation between owner and dog, as happens when a dog is given up to a rescue centre, it seems to set back the process and the dog is likely to develop separation problems in their next home.

New dogs will often follow their owners from room to room at first, even when they go to the bathroom, not wanting to be out of sight in case they should be left behind. This is a perfectly normal response of any social animal to adversity. In the wild, it makes sense to stay with other members of your group when life is dangerous as you have more chance of survival. Consequently, when all your surroundings are new and you are not sure how safe life is, it is sensible to stay with other members of your new pack.

SYMPTOMS

Over-attached dogs want to stay with you. They follow you obsessively when you are in the house and, in severe cases, may want to be in physical contact with you most of the time. Or they may not want to go to sleep unless they are resting against you so they can be ready to follow when you move. If they do become separated from you, they begin to panic and show all the usual symptoms of fear, such as an increased heart rate, dilated pupils, rapid panting and increased activity. This panic tends to subside after the first few minutes, but they will often remain anxious until reunited with you. Dogs that are anxious when left will not want to eat. Chews and food left down will remain untouched until you return.

When left alone in the house, different dogs will cope in different ways. Some may try to scratch and chew at doors and frames, others try to dig through carpet under a door and some become very active and jump up on tables and window sills to look for a way out. Most of the damage is usually concentrated around doorways and windows. If a dog does get out, it will run until it finds someone to be with. Some will bark or howl and some will become so upset that their need to go to the toilet is so great that they go in the house. Some will do nothing but sit and shake and some do all of the above. Whatever the symptoms, this problem begins as soon as you leave the house. As dogs begin to learn your routine, you will find that they begin to get agitated as you begin your preparations for departure.

Dogs that are over-attached to their owners will want to be with you all of the time. They will try to follow you and may bark or chew when they find they cannot.

Teach your dog to tolerate being alone

The only solution is to gradually desensitise your dog to being left alone. You will need to begin very slowly with very short periods of separation and gradually build up to leaving him for longer. In extreme cases you will need to begin with getting your dog to accept being away from you when you are in the same room, but most dogs can tolerate this without a problem. For most dogs, being shut in another room while the new owner is in another is the first step. Doing this throughout the day, starting with, perhaps, 20 one-minute separations will begin the process. Gradually increase the isolation period until he can cope alone while you are in the house for up to one hour. Then begin again, but this time leave the house completely. Again, gradually build up until your dog can cope with two or more hours alone.

Throughout this process, never go faster than your dog can cope with. If you leave him so long that he begins to get agitated, you will be setting back your progress. Go slowly and you will soon begin to achieve results. If you have to leave him for a longer period, try to find someone who can look after him during that time. If you can do this, you will achieve the end result much more quickly.

AN ATTITUDE THAT WORKS

Over-attached dogs get worse if you give them attention constantly when you are with them. The contrast between you being there and not being there will be so great that the dog finds it very difficult to cope alone. For this reason, it helps to give attention in doses rather than in a continuous trickle. Set aside five or 10 minutes in every hour for undivided attention and play. Make a lot of fuss of your dog during this time, but for the rest of the hour ignore him completely unless you need to interact with him for another purpose. In this way, he gets the same amount of attention, but it is given in a different way on your terms. Since he has to cope without you to some degree when you are there, it will make it easier for him to cope when he is alone.

For the same reason, say any goodbyes at least half an hour before you leave. When the time comes, just walk out the door with a minimum of disturbance. If you make a big fuss of him before you leave, there will be too great a contrast between you being there and not, which will make it more difficult for him to cope without you.

Separation problems due to fear

Fear of things outside or inside the house is another reason why dogs may be worried about being left alone. Such dogs are usually able to cope with the fear only when owners are present, but when they are left alone they begin to panic.

A classic example is a dog that is frightened of thunder. During a thunderstorm, a phobic dog left alone will panic and may try to 'go to ground' to get away from the noise. It may run around frantically and go to the toilet in the house in its distress. It may dig into a carpet under a table, try to get into a cupboard, dig into a sofa or mattress or hide under a bed. Dogs that have not experienced thunder when outside may think the noise comes from the house itself. These dogs will try to get out of the house and will damage doorways and windows.

OTHER TIPS TO HELP WITH SEPARATION PROBLEMS

- Leave a scarf that you have been wearing recently on the outside handle of the door through which you exit. Your dog will sniff under the door to find out if you are still close and may be reassured by your scent.
- Leave a radio playing or a tape recording of family activity. This may help block out other noises that may cause your dog to worry and may provide a more familiar background sound in the house.
- Feed your dog a small meal a short time before leaving so he will be more sleepy.
- Leave your dog in the place where he will feel most secure, but where he can do least damage. Keep him away from valuable items and furniture and anything that may damage him, such as electrical wires. Leaving him in the centre of the house may help him to feel more secure and, if he barks or whines, may limit the noise that your neighbours can hear.
- Leave your dog inside the house rather than outside. Leaving him outside will make him more insecure and will make the problem worse. It will also make it more likely that he will bark and upset your neighbours.

Scared dogs often try to find a dark, safe place when left alone and may chew up items that carry your scent.

FEAR OF THINGS OUTSIDE THE HOUSE

Dogs can be frightened of a whole range of things that may worry them while their owner is away. They may be worried about other dogs or people entering the house – they don't know the door is locked – or unfamiliar noises outside. It may be a constant fear that lasts all the time the owners are away or it may be triggered by certain events such as the postman delivering letters. This type of problem may therefore occur every time your dog is left alone or it may happen sporadically when triggered by an external event. It may occur immediately because he is anticipating being scared and is getting worried about being left or it may be triggered by an event later.

Dogs that are afraid of things coming into the house from outside may take objects that smell of their owner, chew them up into small pieces and curl up in the debris so they are surrounded by a nest of their owner's scent. Being such scent-oriented animals, one can only assume that they think other animals and people will smell the scent of the pack leader and go away and leave other pack members alone. They will often choose the items that smell most strongly of their owners, such as the TV remote control, underwear, the arm of a favourite chair or other items recently touched or worn. They will often select items that carry the scent of the person in the household who they perceive to be the strongest.

Another way dogs may cope with their fear of things coming into the house is to mark their territory with urine. If your dog does this, you will often find that strategic points in the house have been marked. These are specially positioned so that an intruder cannot fail to walk past them as they enter. The dog is hopeful that the 'intruder' will smell his presence, appreciate that they are on someone else's territory and go away.

FEAR OF THINGS INSIDE

Dogs may also be worried about noises that occur within the house, such as fridges or heating switching on and off, wind in the chimney or cellar or noises from next door. These dogs will try to get out of the house if they can and will damage doors and windows as they attempt to do this. If they do get out they will often sit on the doorstep waiting for you to get back rather than run away.

TREATMENT

The key lies in discovering exactly what such a dog is afraid of and desensitising him to it. It is not always easy to find the cause, particularly if it is something that happens inside the house. You could leave a tape or video recorder running when you go out to help you to detect noises and movements and find out when the problem begins so you may be able to link it to some external occurrence. You could also leave your dog in a different room to find out where he is less worried, but this could lead to more damage in rooms previously untouched.

Once you have found out what it is that scares him try to desensitise him to it. You will need to do this slowly and, preferably, he will need to be left with someone until he has got over his fears. Introduce him very slowly to a reduced form of whatever it is that scares him and make sure he has a happy experience with it by playing with his favourite toys and feeding him exciting treats. Gradually increase the amount of exposure he gets to the frightening thing, never going beyond what he can cope with, until he is happy and coping in its presence. When he is no longer frightened, it will be safe to leave him alone again. For dogs that are afraid of people or other dogs, a gradual socialisation programme will be needed to make him more settled in their presence (see page 105).

TIP

Never leave anxious dogs shut into an indoor kennel as they can cause terrible damage to their paws and mouth in their panic to get out.

FIRST AID MEASURES

Until you have found the cause of the fear, there are various first aid measures that can help should you have to leave your dog alone. For a dog with mild problems, these may be all that is necessary for him to feel calm again.

● Leave a large article of clothing, preferably made from natural fibre, which you have recently worn for your dog to curl up in. Only leave something that you do not mind being chewed! Leave it where he is most likely to lie while you are out. To find out where your dog likes to lie, feel for the warm patch on the floor or furniture when you return. Replenish your scent on the clothing each time you go out – wear it again, rub it on your skin or keep it in the laundry basket with your dirty clothes.

● If your dog urinates in the house, put down pieces of kitchen towel down, which you have wiped on your own skin, in the areas he has marked in the past.
If he continues to mark these areas, put polythene down so it is at least easy to clean up.

● It may help to provide your dog with a den-like area for him to crawl into to feel safe. A strong cardboard box may work or try an indoor kennel with a blanket over it and the door left open. Put the 'den' under a table or in the place where your dog lies when you are out. You may also be able to cover a table with a blanket to provide a small, dark place for your dog to go when he is scared.

● Exercise your dog well in advance of leaving him so he has time to settle down again before you go out.

DRUG THERAPY

There are drugs available through veterinary surgeons that can help some dogs with very severe cases of anxiety. However, these do need to be used in conjunction with treatment recommended by a pet behaviour counsellor. If your dog has a very severe problem when left alone, ask your veterinary surgeon to refer you to a good pet behaviour counsellor in your area.

Bored dogs

Young dogs or those with lots of energy will become bored when left alone for too long and will often find unacceptable ways to fill their time. These dogs will often lie down for a sleep as soon as you have gone so there will be a certain delay before their problem behaviour starts. Bored dogs are most likely to chew, although some will bark, usually at the slightest disturbance, just for something to do. If they chew, they are likely to select loose objects or they may choose items made

Leave plenty of things for active dogs to do when you leave them on their own.

Dogs are scavengers by nature. They will not think it is 'wrong' to raid the bin while you are out, but are following an innate drive to take food while they can.

from the same material, such as wood, plastic or upholstery.

Dogs most prone to these sorts of separation problems are young dogs with lots of energy, particularly those aged between six and 10 months. This is a time when dogs would naturally leave their nest site to explore their envirnoment. Keeping them confined at this time with little to do makes it likely that they will find their own ways to occupy themselves, often with their teeth around your house!

Breeds that were bred to work, and their crosses, often find it extremely difficult to lie down all day with nothing to do. They often have too much mental and physical energy for a sedentary life and some dogs can become quite disturbed if kept in such restricted conditions. Gundogs, especially labradors, were bred to use their mouths and are particularly likely to chew.

WHAT TO DO WITH BORED DOGS

Give energetic dogs much more mental and physical activity when you are at home. Plenty of off lead running is necessary for young, active dogs so teach them to come back when called and take them to a place where it is safe for them to run free at least twice a day. Equally important is the need to use up their mental energy. Do this by playing with toys as often as possible. Train them to respond to commands, to do tricks and to be useful around the house by fetching named items. Teach them to play games such as 'find the hidden toy' so that they can exercise while you sit back and relax. Rather than feeding them all their food in one dish, hide it in pots placed in different locations around the house so that they can search them out while you have gone. Try to be inventive about the things you do with your dog while you are at home and you will find that he is more content to lie down and do nothing while you are away.

THINK AHEAD

- Stuff strong toys and bones with food, such as biscuits, meat paste or cream cheese, to make them more interesting once the novelty begins to wear off. Toys are not much fun if a dog has to play with them by himself for long periods, so find ways to make them more interesting. A strong, solid ball can be drilled with small holes and filled with dry, pelleted food.
- Try to arrange for someone to visit your dog during the day if you can to break up the monotony.
- Exercise your dog well just before you leave and play with him so that he is both physically and mentally tired.
- Restrict your dog's access to valuable items or put them up out of his reach until he has learned to play with his toys and chews only.
- Put a low table or chair under a window for your dog to sit on. Some dogs are happier if they can see out of a window and watch what is going on outside and this will help relieve some of the boredom of a long day alone.
- You may like to find out if it would be possible to take your dog to work with you. This will give you added incentive to train him to behave well so that he would fit easily into your workplace.

You may have to introduce a new dog to a different routine from the one he was used to in the rescue centre. If you find your dog sleeps all evening and is active during the day, encourage him to be active when you are at home so that he is inactive when you leave him. Leave things for your dog to play with and chew while you are out. Gather at least 20 items together that he can play with and chew (there is an enormous range available in shops). Two different toys can be left down each day and not used again for a over week if you have 20. Pick toys up when you return home so that they stay interesting.

Dogs not used to living in houses

Some dogs will not be used to living in a house and will need to be taught how to behave before being left alone. Their natural tendency to explore can otherwise lead them into all sorts of trouble while you are not there to correct them. Do not leave them alone in a place where they can damage expensive items or chew through cables until they have learned how to behave.

To teach a dog how to behave well in your absence, keep him under close supervision during your early days together and correct him when he does something that is inappropriate. The best way to do this is to throw something soft and heavy, such as a cushion, so it lands on him just as he is beginning to engage in the undesirable activity. It should not hurt him, but it should unsettle him enough to put him off the activity next time. If the cushion appears to come out of the blue rather than from you, he is likely to connect the small fright with the activity itself rather than you. He is therefore unlikely to do it again even if you are not in the house at the time.

It is important to offer him something that he is allowed to chew a few minutes later. He will be in the mood for chewing or exploring and you can use this opportunity to teach him what he can chew. When he settles down to chew the offered item, praise him well. By repeating this procedure consistently during the first few weeks together your dog will gradually learn that it is not a good idea to chew anything other than the items you want him to chew.

Dogs can be taught to lie down and rest until you return. Make sure they are well exercised and comfortable before leaving.

CHAPTER

9

Curing Minor Behaviour Problems

It is likely that you will encounter some behaviour problems with your new dog as he adjusts to his new lifestyle. Some of these will be very minor and will cure themselves eventually as he settles in, but others will be more difficult and I have included a selection of the more common problems to give you some guidance on what to do.

If you cannot solve your dog's behaviour problem alone, a Pet Behaviour Counsellor can provide experienced, practical help and advice.

General rules

I have been able to include the basics of each cure only as space is limited in a book, but I hope some of it will be useful to help deal with those difficult teething troubles in the early days.

CHECK YOUR DOG'S HEALTH FIRST

Some behaviour problems are caused by an underlying medical problem and it is wise to take your new dog for a health check at your veterinary surgery before you do anything else. A dog that refuses to sit or lie down when asked, for example, or that is reluctant to move, is grumpy in the mornings or bites when picked up could have painful joints or be tender in a certain place. Some conditions, such as, epilepsy can cause mood changes that can result in erratic bad behaviour. Unusual behaviour is the first symptom for many ailments and, for a mild condition, it could be the only symptom. A health check will give peace of mind and is a necessary requirement before you see a professional behaviour counsellor.

FIND EXPERT HELP FOR SEVERE PROBLEMS

Many people profess to be experts when it comes to solving dog behaviour problems and you will receive advice from many quarters. You will need to find someone who has a considerable amount of both practical experience of dealing with dogs and the necessary academic training and knowledge to help solve behaviour problems. It is becoming easier to find such people now that pet behaviour therapy is becoming more widespread. Write to the Association of Pet Behaviour Counsellors (see page 158) or ask your veterinary surgeon for a referral.

WILL PUNISHMENT WORK?

If your dog is behaving in an unacceptable way, you will need to act to prevent it happening again. The natural human reaction is to punish. In some cases, it will be possible to inhibit a behaviour by the use of punishment, but in the majority the motivation behind the behaviour will remain and it is likely to be exhibited again, and maybe when you have less control.

If your dog tries an unwanted behaviour again you are likely to escalate the punishment and sooner or later you could be using severe punishment out of all proportion to the 'crime'. Worse still, punishment can quickly lead to resentment and a break-down of the relationship you were building up. Punishment is rarely as successful as we would like to think it is and a more intelligent approach will bring greater benefits and a quicker resolution to the problem.

Your dog may be behaving badly because one or more of his basic needs are not being met.

THE 'INTELLIGENT' APPROACH TO PROBLEM SOLVING

Try to find out why your dog does what he does. Finding the motivation behind a behaviour pattern is crucial for deciding on the correct course of action. Try to decide what is motivating your dog to do what he does. Think what it is about the bad behaviour that he finds rewarding. Once you know this, you can arrange for him to receive rewards in a different way so that he changes his behaviour.

SATISFY YOUR DOG'S NEEDS

Before attempting to cure a behaviour problem take another look at the special species needs in Chapter 5. Many problems arise because your dog's needs are not being met. If you suspect one of these needs is not catered for sufficiently, it will be easier to rectify this rather than focus on the problem itself. For example, if your dog barks excessively at every little sound in an attempt to 'entertain' himself because he is not receiving enough mental and physical exercise, it is easier to provide for that need than to attempt to stop the behaviour. Provide adequately for your dog's special species needs and the unwanted behaviour will be easily prevented or discouraged

In addition, look at the relationship you have with your dog before attempting to cure behaviour problems. Does your dog respect you? Is he willing to do things for you easily? Does he

Providing your dog with more play and exercise will help to ensure that he settles down more easily when he is inside the house.

look to you for support? Does he feel loved by you and part of your social group? If the answer to these questions is yes, you have a good basis for solving behaviour problems. If you are so cross with him because of his behaviour that you find you do not like him very much or you are thinking of returning him you are almost certainly doomed to fail unless you can change your attitude. Dogs know if they are loved and supported and those that are unwanted display all sorts of difficult behaviour that will not disappear until they feel part of the pack once more.

Dogs that are generally disobedient or do not pay attention often have a less-than-perfect relationship with their owners. Your dog will listen to you only if he respects you and if he wants to please you. Look again at the pack leadership rules (see page 69) and try to develop a more structured relationship with your dog.

Jumping up

Dogs jump up so that they can reach your face and have maximum social contact with you. This has its origins in puppy greeting behaviour which involves licking the muzzle of returning adults who might be bringing food for them. They consider it a compliment, whereas we, who get scratched, knocked over or covered in muddy paw prints, consider it a nuisance.

Turning away from a dog that is jumping up makes his behaviour less rewarding.

To cure this behaviour, you have to make it unrewarding and, when your dog offers an alternative greeting reward this instead. You either need to ignore the jumping up or prevent it from happening. Ignore the jumping up and turn away so your dog is presented with your back rather than your face to prevent him from being rewarded by this behaviour. Do not speak to, look at or touch him while he is jumping. Alternatively for a large, boisterous dog or one with a very bad habit, hold his collar as soon as you meet him and use it to hold him down as he jumps to prevent him coming up. As soon as your dog has all four feet on the ground and has stopped jumping, bend over or crouch down so he can greet you properly without needing to jump.

If everyone in your family acts consistently, you will find that he will eventually begin to realise that he can greet you more quickly by staying on the floor. At first, you may find that he tries harder to reach you if you are ignoring him, but if you persist, he will soon realise that this behaviour is no longer rewarding.

It is important to restrain your dog so he does not jump on children or visitors. Hold his collar and ask everyone to ignore him until he has settled. One way to make sure he is not going to jump is to ask him to sit. As soon as he is in the sitting position, they should greet him. If he gets up, they should remove their attention until he sits again.

For dogs with a very bad habit, it is a good idea to set up training times with family or friends. They come in through the front door, go through a training procedure with you and your dog where correct behaviour, ie sitting, is rewarded and leave through the back door and begin again. The excitement will gradually subside and it will become easier to teach him how to behave. Several of these sessions will be needed before he shows the new behaviour instead of jumping up and it will take many, many repetitions before you reach the final goal. Remember that dogs learn sets of associations and teaching him to greet people properly at the front door will need to be repeated in different places if it is to become second nature to him everywhere.

Problems at night

If your dog cannot be left alone during the day, he is unlikely to cope when left alone at night. Rather than risk sleepless nights, it may be better to let him sleep outside your bedroom until he feels more at home. This may seem like 'giving in' to him, but if the problem is caused by his anxiety about being alone there is nothing to be gained from forcing him to be alone too quickly. When he is more comfortable about being left alone during the day (see pages 116 to 120), you can begin to move him away from you at night until he sleeps where you want him to sleep.

NOT CLEAN AT NIGHT
If your dog is not house-trained, you will need to ensure you go through the training procedure at night (see page 136). If your dog is clean during the day unless you leave him on his own, you have a separation problem to cope with (see page 118). Dogs that go to the toilet soon after being left are more likely to have a separation problem than those that hang on until just before you get up in the mornings.

Some dogs are house-trained by day and confident about being left alone, but have got into the habit of going to the toilet inside at night. They may have developed this habit in kennels, they may be more relaxed at night or their feeding pattern is such

DRY FOOD

If you feed your dog dry food in the evening, soak it beforehand or feed it with added water. Otherwise your dog will be very thirsty and will drink a lot of water. This excess water will need to come out during the night so your dog will either end up disturbing you in an effort to go outside or will urinate on the floor.

INCONTINENCE

Some spayed bitches can become incontinent and may leak urine when lying down. If your female dog's bedding is wet in the mornings, seek advice from your veterinary surgeon who will provide appropriate treatment.

that they need to go at night. Other dogs will not go to the toilet outside for some reason and do not want to go to the toilet in front of you.

Whatever the reason, the easiest way to solve the problem is to take your dog into your bedroom at night and confine him to his bed so that he cannot get out. Few dogs will soil their own bed so if he wakes up in the middle of the night and makes a fuss take him into the garden and wait with him until he goes to the toilet. Praise him if he does, bring him back inside and put him back to bed. Going to the toilet in this way will be inconvenient for him and he will soon acclimatise his body to going in the morning instead. Continue this regime until you have a week of undisturbed nights before putting him back in his regular sleeping place. Confine him to his bed during the night for a further week, but leave doors open and go to him if you hear him making a noise.

House-training

Your new dog may not have lived in a house before or he may have forgotten about being clean in the house and will need reminding. If he has been kept in kennels for any length of time, he will be used to going to the toilet on a hard surface. Once in a home, he may try to use the kitchen floor or patio as his toilet and he will need to be taught to use an alternative place.

A dog that is not house-trained will select a few areas in the house to use as a toilet and will return to these sites again and again. He will usually sneak away to go to the toilet rather than go in front of humans because he will probably have been punished for going in the house in front of humans in the past. This type of punishment does not teach a dog to go outside, it simply teaches him that it is dangerous to go in front of humans. Such a dog will often go to the toilet inside after coming back from a walk, which will stimulate his body. This is particularly annoying, but in the dog's mind he is being very clean by waiting until he could use his toilet.

HOW TO HOUSE-TRAIN AN ADULT DOG

It is quite easy to house-train an adult dog and you will be able to establish new, good habits fairly quickly. Exactly how quickly, however, will depend on how well you can keep to a routine, how fast your dog learns, how old he is and his previous experiences.

STICK TO A ROUTINE

House-training will happen more easily if you keep to the same routine of feeding and exercising each day. A good routine will help your dog establish a regular toileting pattern, which will help you judge the best time to take him outside.

A new dog may take a few weeks to establish a new habit, especially if he has been in kennels for a long time.

Before beginning your new routine, clean all previously soiled areas with biological washing solution or a special cleaner available from your veterinary surgeon. This will remove smells that attract your dog back to the same place each time.

It is important that you keep your dog under constant supervision for a few weeks so he cannot go to the toilet in the house. When you cannot supervise him or when you are asleep he should be confined so he cannot get out of his bed. This will ensure he has no alternative but to go to the toilet in your presence and you can then begin to teach him where you want him to go. Very few dogs will soil their own bed and although it is unfair to confine them there for any longer than a couple of hours, it does prevent them from sneaking off when you are not concentrating and perpetuating bad habits. You will need to either put barricades around the bed or secure your dog so he cannot get out. Never use a check chain and ensure your dog cannot hurt himself when he is tied up. Keep him confined to his bed as little as possible and never for longer than two hours at any one time.

Take your dog outside and let him run around and sniff when you first wake up, last thing at night and every two hours during the day. Both movement and sniffing seem to stimulate dogs to

Reward any obvious sign that your dog makes when he wants to go outside and he will soon be asking to go whenever he needs to.

go to the toilet. Place any soiled newspaper or faeces where you want him to go so the smell will encourage him to go there.

Stay with him and be patient. If he starts to relieve himself, praise him quietly and reward him with a game or food treat when he has finished. If, after five minutes, he has not done anything, take him inside and try again later, but watch him carefully in the meantime.

Keep an eye on him when you are in the house at all times and be aware of what he is doing. If you see your dog about to relieve himself, shout a loud 'No!' and encourage him to run outside with you immediately. Praise him for doing so as it is essential that he associates going outside with a reward. If you catch him in time he will still need to go to the toilet so wait until he is relaxed and praise him well when he has been.

Do not punish your dog for an 'accident' you may discover too late. Consider it to be your fault for not supervising him enough. The easiest solution at night is to position your dog's bed just outside your bedroom door and confine him to it. If you hear him being very restless or if he begins to make a noise, take him outside (see page 136).

If you have to leave the house for longer than two hours during the housetraining period, do not confine your dog to his bed. Instead, ensure he has a chance to exercise and relieve himself before you go out and cover as much of the floor as possible with a large sheet of polythene with newspaper on top. This will not teach him to be clean, but it will make any messes easier to clean up. Do not punish him if he goes to the toilet while you are out. Simply put him in another room until you have cleared it up and try not to leave him for so long in future.

HOW LONG WILL IT TAKE?

You will need to continue this routine for at least two weeks. During this time, your dog will develop a new habit of going outside and will begin to want to go outside whenever he feels the need to go. After two weeks, gradually increase the time between visits to the garden and watch for any sign that he wants to go out. He may become more active or may wander over to the door. Reward this instantly by praising and taking him outside. Once you have reached this stage, you can begin to relax, stop confining him and give him more freedom in the house. Eventually, you will notice specific signals that indicate that he wants to go out, such as running to the door or standing beside it whining. Reinforce these by letting him out and he will soon be asking to go out whenever he needs to go to the toilet. If you always reward these signals with freedom to the garden, he will soon be asking to go out whenever he needs to go to the toilet.

OTHER HOUSE-SOILING PROBLEMS

As well as not being house-trained, some dogs are not clean in the house because of other reasons such as too much stress and tension in the household, anxiety about being left alone and because they are territory marking. Each of these problems will need a different solution other than basic house-training. Each problem will also have other distinct symptoms.

Stressed dogs, for example, will often leave piles of faeces in very obvious places rather than somewhere relatively hidden. They are also more likely to leave them at night. Dogs that are anxious when left will be unclean only when they are left alone. These dogs often produce many small, runny piles rather than one firm one and they may run about in it in their distress. Dogs that are territory marking will also soil in obvious places as they are trying to leave a smelly message for you, visitors or other animals. They will often mark prominent items in a room, entry and exit points and new objects. Curing such behaviour will depend on diagnosing the cause of the problem accurately. Once you have done this the treatment can be fairly straightforward. Seek further help from your vet or a pet behaviour counsellor if you are unable to work out why your dog is behaving in this way.

Excessive barking

Dogs that bark a lot are a nuisance to owners and neighbours. They give dogs a bad name and it is important that you stop the noise before you get complaints from others. There are many reasons why dogs bark too much. Many bark excessively because at some point in their lives all their species needs were not being met and they learned to bark as a way of coping with their frustration. Some will bark whenever they get excited, some may be trying too hard to protect the house and some will bark at their owners to attract attention.

BARKING THROUGH FRUSTRATION OR EXCITEMENT

To discover whether your dog is barking out of excitement or frustration, first ensure you are meeting all his species needs (see chapter 5). Check especially that he has an outlet for mental and physical energy if he is young or particularly active. Giving a dog a job to do in the form of play and other tasks can calm an excitable dog considerably. Teach a good immediate response to the 'sit' or 'down' commands – few dogs will bark when stationary and if your dog responds to these requests, he will often stop barking too, giving you two reasons to reward him well. If he continues to bark even when stationary, you can try teaching him to hold a toy in his mouth as it is difficult for a dog to hold something and bark.

Alternatively, you could teach your dog to bark and be quiet on command. This may seem counterproductive, but it is surprising how many noisy dogs are more quiet once they have learned to bark on command. It is as if they barked without thinking before, but once taught to do it when asked, they seem to be more aware of what they are doing and often stop. If you can teach your dog to bark on command, it is just as easy to teach him to be quiet. Your command may not work at first when he is very excited, but his response should get better in time, particularly if you reinforce your request with one hand on his collar and the other gently holding his mouth closed. Practise this command in different situations.

TERRITORIAL BARKING

Dogs that bark a lot because they are protecting the house and garden from every possible intruder need to meet more people so that they become more sociable. Take them out and about more often so that they do not see their little piece of territory as the end of their world. It is also important to prevent dogs that like to do this all day from running up and down the boundaries. If your dog does this, stop him quickly every time it happens by calling him to you and rewarding him well for coming. If you can, prevent it from happening in the first place and give him something else to do instead.

BARKING FOR ATTENTION

Some dogs will have learned that the only way to attract their owner's attention is to bark at them. These dogs will often stand directly in front of you while you watch TV or are engaged in

Dogs that show aggression when in the car often have a deep-rooted mistrust of strangers.

TEACHING DOGS TO BARK AND BE QUIET ON COMMAND

Fasten your dog to a solid object and step away from him, holding up something he wants. Wave it in front of him and try to generate as much excitement as possible. As soon as he makes any noise at all, even if it is just a whine, throw him his reward and praise him well. Some dogs make a noise more quickly than others, but persist and it is likely that you will eventually get some sort of noise from your dog. Repeat this exercise, gradually waiting for more and more of a noise before throwing the reward.

Introduce the word 'speak!' or 'talk' after a few sessions so that he begins to associate the word with the noise he is making. Continue to practise this for a while, until you can get him to bark on command in any location.

● To teach him to be quiet, again fasten him to a solid object and ask him to bark. This time, do not throw the reward but, instead, after a few moments, ask him to be 'Quiet!'. Use a hand signal to accompany this request to help him to

understand what you want. Wait until he is quiet, even if this takes a long time. As soon as he stops barking, throw him his reward and praise him. Repeat often and gradually build up as before until he responds at once to requests to bark and be quiet.
● Barking is more obvious and easier to reward than periods of quiet so be sure to spend more time asking for and rewarding quiet behaviour during your later training sessions since this is the behaviour you want to encourage.

something else and bark until you direct your attention to them. The only way to deal with your dog if he behaves in this way is to completely ignore him and never reward such behaviour. Everyone in your family needs to do this and you should warn your neighbours that you are about to try to break his habit.

Be prepared for an initial increase in the barking as your dog tries harder with a behaviour that used to work. Eventually he will give up and go and lie down. After a few moments of quiet everyone in the room must reward him with plenty of attention. If he begins to bark with excitement at this point, withdraw the attention again. He will gradually realise that barking does not work, but if he is quiet he will get all the attention he needs. This method needs perseverance, but it is guaranteed to work if you never reward your dog for barking for attention again.

Bad manners

Some dogs may not have lived inside a house before and will need to be taught how to behave properly. Sharing your home with a dog that has not lived as a pet before or with one that was allowed to get away with bad behaviour can be very difficult at first. These dogs will require an enormous amount of effort initially but you should begin to see results after a few days if you persevere.

Insist on good behaviour at all times. If necessary, physically prevent your dog from doing something wrong. Take control and show him what you want him to do so it does not become a continuous battle where you run around behind him telling him off. You can then reward him for doing the right thing and both of you will be satisfied. Initially, it may help to confine him to one room if his behaviour is very disruptive, but give him many outings into the rest of the house each day, whenever you are able to make a small amount of time available to teach him appropriate behaviour.

Make sure your dog does not barge through gates and doors ahead of you. Insisting on good manners from the outset will get your dog into good habits and make him more respectful.

ENVIRONMENTAL CORRECTION

As well as physically preventing bad behaviour, you can also use a technique called environmental correction to help him learn that there are some things he should not do. If your dog is about to jump up onto a table to eat from a plate of food, for example, throw something soft and heavy at him just as he is thinking about jumping up. The timing is crucial as once he has been rewarded by reaching the food, it is too late. If he is thinking about jumping and preparing to leap when the object lands, you will have got the timing just right. Throw the object so it makes him jump and move away from the area. It should not scare him so much that he runs away, but neither should it be so soft that he continues with what he is doing.

Alternative 'corrections' are to throw something that makes a loud noise towards him, such as a can with pebbles inside or a bunch of keys. It will be more effective if the 'correction' comes out of the blue so it should not appear to come from you. If you get it right and the 'correction' does not appear to come from you, it will be an effective deterrent from repeating the same behaviour even if you are not present. You will need several repetitions of this in different places before your dog decides that eating food from surfaces is not a good idea.

Car travel

Many owners experience problems when travelling in a car with their dog and if you intend to do a lot of travelling, how your dog behaves in the car is something you should check first. Problems can range from car sickness to frantic barking and ripping up seats. As with all problems, there is always a reason behind such behaviour and you will need to find out what it is before the problem can be solved.

CAR SICKNESS AND FEAR

Some dogs have genuine motion sickness – these dogs will often be fine on short journeys, but will become sick if they are in the car for longer periods. Many dogs, however, are just afraid of being in a car when it is moving and it is this fear that makes them sick. Such dogs will often begin to drool and look uncomfortable as soon as the car begins to move. They are likely to be sick quite soon after you have begun your journey. Other dogs may shake, whine or bark and some may even go the toilet in their distress. Dogs that bark because they are afraid will only

Dogs that leap around and bark when the car is moving are a nuisance and can be dangerous if they distract the driver.

do so when the car is moving. It will be worse if you are travelling fast, but it tends to settle down when on motorways.

If your dog is afraid of car motion, you need to desensitise him slowly. This will mean taking him on very short journeys at first, all of which end in a walk or a fun and rewarding event. The length of the journey should depend on your dog's fear levels. Gradually increase the journey times over the following weeks, taking care not to overwhelm your dog with too much too soon. If your dog barks because he is afraid, it will be easy to tell if you are taking things too fast.

Drive carefully, try to avoid bumps and take corners slowly. Placing your dog in a different part of the car may also help. If you have ever travelled in the dog compartment at the rear of an estate car, you will realise how bumpy it is and how it must be difficult for dogs, to keep their footing. Teach him to sit quietly in the front footwell or just behind the passenger seat. Be sure to confine him carefully at first so he cannot interfere with your driving and cause an accident.

CHASING

Some dogs have descended from dogs bred for herding and their desire to chase moving objects gets them into trouble when travelling in a car. These dogs will focus on objects coming towards them such as trees, people or other dogs, will bark frantically as they get closer and then spin round as they pass ready to 'chase' the next thing. In extreme cases, such dogs may also tear at upholstery in their frustration at not being able to run after the object.

These dogs will often bark only as the car speeds up and objects move past the car fast enough to trigger the excitement. To cure such a dog it is necessary to teach him to lie down so his head is below the level of the window or confine him to a covered travelling cage so he cannot see out. Ensure he has adequate opportunity to direct his chase energies into acceptable games with toys when he is outside.

FEAR OF THINGS OUTSIDE THE CAR

Dogs that are afraid other people, children, lorries or other animals will often bark at them when they see them from the car window. You will need to desensitise such as dog to his fear (see chapter 7), but a short-term solution is to restrict his view of the outside world using a covered travel cage so he cannot be scared by things passing by.

EXCITEMENT IN THE CAR

Some dogs will bark with excitement because most of their car journeys end in a walk or something else exciting. If your dog does this, take him on more boring journeys, which do not involve getting out, to lessen the excitement. It is also helpful to make him wait for 10 minutes or so at the end of each journey before allowing him out. When you do get him out, keep him walking to heel and doing slow exercises for a while before letting him free. Ensure that he is getting plenty of activity to use up his energies and play a long energetic game with him in the garden to use up any excess energy before loading him into the car.

ATTENTION SEEKING

Dogs that bark to attract their owner's attention at home are likely to do it in the car too, especially if they are prevented from reaching their owners by a dog guard. These dogs will look at the back of their owner's head and bark continuously until they are spoken to. Cure this problem at home (see page 140) before confining yourself in the car with him where you will find it hard to ignore the behaviour.

CAR TRAVEL TIPS

- Keep trips short at first.
- Follow up car journeys with a pleasurable walk or game if your dog dreads journeys or tire him out with a walk or energetic game beforehand if he gets overexcited.
- Drive steadily and avoid bumps.
- Move your dog from the rear of the car to behind the front passenger seat or in the passenger well to see if this calms him.
- Make sure your dog is secure and cannot interfere with you or the car controls.
- Try putting your dog in a covered travelling cage if he is afraid of things outside or likes to 'chase' objects that pass by.

Running away

Your new dog may have run away from his previous home on a regular basis. This will have taught him about the benefits of exploring farther afield. He may run off to find other people or dogs to play with, he may go hunting or he may be looking for a mate. Ensuring he (or she) is neutered will help with the latter, but dogs that run away often do so because their species needs are not being met. They are probably not being given enough to do to use up their energy or may not be given enough social contact.

If you acquire such a dog, it is important that you keep him physically restrained until you have developed a stronger bond with him and he realises how beneficial it is to live with you. Unless you have very secure fences, keep a long line attached to a point near the door and attach the other end to his collar whenever you let him free in the garden. Pay particular attention to not letting him escape through the main door, ensure he has a collar and tag and have him microchipped just in case. Eventually, if you are being a good owner and meeting all his needs, he should have no need to run away and will be content to stay around you.

Dogs can get through suprisingly small spaces if they are really determined.

CHAPTER

10

Beau's Story

When I first acquired Beau, a labrador/weimeraner cross, he was 18 months old and had bitten at least eight people. He would threaten anyone who walked too close, was aggressive to all dogs and other animals, was very domineering, pulled hard on the lead and, generally, was a mixed up and difficult dog. At the time of writing he is now 11 years old. He has visited elderly patients in hospitals as part of the Pets as Therapy dog scheme, has competed in agility and working trial competitions, is loving with everyone he meets, good with other animals and children and is, generally, my perfect adopted dog. His story is included here to give hope to those of you who are experiencing behaviour problems with your new adopted dog.

Beau at 18 months old. A very worried dog who was confident his aggression would deter unwanted invaders from his territory.

Beau came to my attention soon after I had begun solving pet behaviour problems for The Blue Cross. He had been out to two homes, had bitten both new owners and had also been aggressive to kennel staff too. The general consensus of opinion was that he could not be homed again to risk another bite and, unless I could do something with him, he would have to be put to sleep. I knew the theory and had had lots of practical experience with difficult dogs over the years, but I had never had to deal with anything quite this bad. I had plenty of doubts about a successful outcome, but since even if I failed to cure him, Beau would have lost nothing, it seemed worth a try. In addition, many staff at The Blue Cross were sceptical about pet behaviour therapy at that time and the desire to prove I could completely change a dog's behaviour gave me added incentive. I also knew that I had one of the best advisors in the world to hand if I needed advice. John Rogerson, who was teaching me more about dog behaviour, was at the other end of the phone if I needed to call him for reassurance and guidance on what to do next.

I decided on the day I would take over Beau's care as I knew he would need to learn to depend on me totally. On the allotted Thursday morning, I stood in front of his kennel and watched his frenzied barking and frothing at the mouth for what seemed like

We used gradual desensitisation and plenty of titbits to overcome Beau's fear of men.

an eternity. If it subsided a little, I would make a movement towards the door and he would begin again in earnest. Rather more frightened of going back in defeat to the kennel staff who were watching with interest from the kitchen window, I decided I would just have to risk it. Going into his kennel that day took more courage than I knew I had. Once I had managed to attach a lead with trembling fingers, he proceeded to take me out for a walk. Half way round, I decided to take back some control so I tightened the lead and told him to sit. He rolled his eyes towards me, gave me a stare that made the hairs on the back of my neck stand on end and lifted his lip ever so slightly to show a sliver of white canine. Determined not to be outdone, I told him firmly to stand still, praised him for doing this and walked on swiftly!

After that we progressed on a daily basis. I put into action all the tricks I knew for subtly reducing a dog's status and avoided confrontation at all cost. I refused to let him beat me in all

encounters, insisting that he do something once I had asked, making sure I could physically make him do it without getting bitten before asking. Quite quickly he seemed to realise he had met his match and began to change his behaviour towards me. Since I was not using aggression of any sort, he quickly began to trust me and we developed a firm friendship. Staff used to comment that he seemed to get smaller after I took him on. This could have been because he was no longer such a threat to them, but I think it had more to do with his lowered tail and body carriage as his status declined to a more reasonable level. At home, his attitude was one of humility once he had been treated to a formidable display of strength and power by Winnie, my Rhodesian ridgeback, who was very definitely in charge of the dogs in the household.

Beau's aggression to other people and animals was more difficult to overcome. He had had quite a lot of rough treatment from previous owners and professionals who should have known better in their efforts to try to control him and, consequently, was afraid of people approaching him. He was more afraid of men than women, so we began with any women who were brave enough to volunteer. I will be forever grateful to the women who worked at The Blue Cross during that time, particularly Tina Kew who took the first brave step of sitting still, eyes averted, hand outstretched offering food. We tried not to hold our breaths during those early encounters, but gradually they began to like and trust each other and, in this way, I was able to gradually increase his circle of friends.

It took about two years before I was able to trust him fully with strangers. This time was not without incident. Once, quite soon after I had taken him on, I had left him in the office on a Saturday morning while I went to help with the Christmas bazaar. One of the men who worked at The Blue Cross went in to my office unexpectedly carrying a big box. Beau leapt up and took the front of the box out with one big bite. I prefer not to think of what may have happened if the box had not been there!

Having a stable home and an owner whom he could trust were as much a part of the cure as the work I was able to do with him with other people. I made sure he was kept away from aggressive, difficult people, and, gradually, he learned to trust again. People came to represent good time and food to him, rather than fear and pain. On one memorable occasion, a group of us were having a coffee break together and one of the temporary staff asked what had happened to that awful, aggressive black dog we had. We all laughed and looked at Beau who was leaning against her enjoying the experience of having his head stroked.

During Beau's rehabilitation, I discovered an interesting test for assessing a dog's level of fear. When I first had him, Beau would make the whole car rock as he threw himself at the windows barking and snarling whenever anyone walked past. Gradually, as he began to change his attitude to people, this behaviour subsided until a stranger would have to go up and put their hands on the car to make it happen. Eventually, he stopped worrying about people all together and now never barks at people unless we see someone particularly suspicious on a dark, quiet road. This concept of showing true feelings when within a small, easily defendable space is now used as part of our assessment of dogs in a kennel environment and we are able to tell a lot more about their true character in this way.

Beau's aggression to dogs was probably caused mostly by lack of early socialisation together with a few attacks that confirmed his impression that all dogs were dangerous. His way of dealing with fear was to try to make himself as large as possible to show the world just how powerful he was. This unfortunate attitude made other dogs react very badly to him, which added to the problem. At the time, I was competing in agility competitions with my spaniel, Sammy. These proved to be an ideal training ground as most agility dogs are used to other dogs and tend to ignore them, as well as being focused on their owners. I would park in the most remote spot in the car park and stay on the edge of the action. If I got too close, Beau would display aggression, but if I got farther away, this would subside to shaking and whining. Gradually, this was replaced with calm behaviour, which I would reward with favourite titbits and lots of praise. This regime was practised whenever we encountered other dogs over the next year and his behaviour began to improve, slowly at first and then more rapidly.

At times, it was tempting to get cross with Beau. Having him try to launch himself at other well behaved dogs was embarrassing and annoying. Sometimes, it was hard to remember that he was afraid, and I would begin to wonder if he was just being difficult. On a few occasions, I shouted at him in frustration and pulled him around to try to stop him. This confused him and made him worse, and I would go home defeated. Reasoning things out when I was more calm, and calling to mind how he shook and cried at agility shows made me more sympathetic and, with a change in my behaviour, we began to make progress.

At the same time, I was gradually introducing him to other friendly dogs that he learned to tolerate and eventually play with. As he slowly began to improve, I began to do agility classes with him too. One day we were waiting our turn to go into the ring. Beau was off lead beside me and I was concentrating on the route we were to take. Seizing the opportunity, a German shepherd dog that always liked to have a go at Beau if he could, lunged out of the waiting group and bit him on the bottom. Instead of spinning round and launching a counter-attack, Beau whirled round to the front of me and sat looking up at the pocket I kept the titbits in, preferring to concentrate on something happy rather than get into a fight. It was then that I knew we had nearly made it. Nowadays, he continues to be a bit awkward with other dogs, but he is never aggressive. If they are difficult with him, he will growl and back off, sometimes coming to find me if he feels things may get out of hand. Such a faith in my abilities is very touching, but perhaps he knows that I would risk serious injury to help him out if he was in real danger.

When I first took Beau home, we had a shy, timid cat. Beau would become transfixed by her whenever she was in the room and would watch her with an unblinking stare, trembling and drooling. Given the chance, he would chase her, but I kept him under very close surveillance so that he was not able to do so. A few weeks after I had begun taking Beau home, I accidentally let him into the room where the cat was without keeping him restrained as I normally did. Beau made a dash for the cat, who raced across the kitchen and jumped up onto the window sill out of danger. I heard Beau's teeth snap together as he sprang up to get her.

Beau grew up with young children and always enjoyed their company. During his early life, they were the only humans he could trust.

I was so angry with him for 'letting me down' that I chased him round the house until I cornered him in the living room. All my training forgotten in the heat of the moment, I raised my hand to smack him. He leapt up, standing on two legs against the wall, eyes tightly shut, making biting movements with his jaws. In an instant, I was ashamed of myself for bringing back all the memories of the terrors he must have experienced in previous homes, and I called him to me and cuddled him. This experience did nothing for his desire to chase the cat which continued for a few more months, but it strengthened the bond of trust between us and made me realise how easily people are driven to use aggression when things are not going according to plan. It is also very easy to ascribe human values to our rescue dogs and to think of them as being 'ungrateful' when they misbehave when in reality they have no such conscience. Gradually, Beau learned to stay put whenever a cat was in the room. If he sees one now, he will not chase it, but he will not take his eyes off it either.

To assist with his overall response to commands, I began to train him to compete in the sport of Working Trials. Since this was mostly for my own entertainment, I decided that I would use positive reinforcement only and never tell him off for doing the wrong thing. As a consequence, it took me a long time to get him good enough to qualify at the Companion Dog and Utility Dog level, but the rewards of working with a dog that loved every minute of the training were worth it. In addition, I learned how much easier and better it is to train using positive methods, which I am now able to pass on to other people to help with their dogs. One of the first things I had to teach him was to retrieve since many of the exercises require dogs to find hidden objects. When I first took him on, he would not play or pick up anything and I had to begin with a small film canister filled with favourite treats. Gradually, we progressed until he would pick up anything, including metal objects. Once, when out in the 'search square' where several objects were hidden, he stood stationary for a few moments, looking intently at the ground. He then leapt high in the air, pounced, and came running back to me looking particularly pleased. I held out my hands to receive the object as usual and he spat out his trophy – a freshly killed, still warm, but very dead mouse.

A few months after I began working with him, I decided not to keep him as I already had two dogs and did not really want a third. I advertised him locally and several suitable people came to look at him. I managed to find a fault with them all and, after a while, someone kindly pointed out that I would never find anyone good enough, no matter how long I looked for the 'perfect' owner. I realised they were right and adopted him officially soon afterwards. Staff at rescue centres have my admiration. They do an incredibly difficult job; looking after and caring for animals, growing attached to them and then letting them go.

Beau and I have come a long way together. He has accompanied me everywhere, particularly to talks and courses that I give where I use his story to teach people how it is possible to change a dog's behaviour. In the early days, when I used to become very scared at the thought of public speaking, Beau would begin to drool when I began to worry and would continue until the talk was over. This outward sign of my fear was a demonstration of our close bond and it was a relief to all when I became more confident. The strength of our relationship was a big factor in Beau's conversion into a good pet dog. It is important for anyone taking on a problem dog to realise how much he or she will need to rely on you during the early stages.

I was lucky because Beau was basically a good dog underneath. By that I mean that his genetic makeup gave him a temperament that was neither too reactive nor too prone to developing irreversible fears. Had he had more collie or herding dog genetics in his makeup, I may never have got him over the early damage his environment inflicted on him.

It is strange to look back on all of this and remember how he used to behave. We have had many problem-free years since that difficult time and it is now hard to imagine life without him. My experience with him has taught me so much about behaviour problems and made me very aware of the plight of other people who take on difficult dogs. If you are having problems with your new dog, or have taken on a challenging dog that is as mixed up as Beau was, I hope his story will give you hope for the future. Get expert help if the problems are severe and remember that changes only happen slowly. Persevere and do not expect good behaviour straight away. If you fail, then you were unlucky, but at least you tried. If you succeed, you will have the pleasure of knowing that you saved a dog from a very uncertain future and you will have a love and loyalty that no money can buy.

Beau during a coffee break at work enjoying the company of the staff at The Blue Cross Centre.

Useful addresses

Association of Pet Behaviour Counsellors
P O Box 46,
Worcester WR8 9YS
Email: apbc@petbcent.demon.co.uk
WWW.apbc.org.uk

Association of Pet Dog Trainers
Peacocks Farm ,
Northchapel,
Petworth,
West Sussex GU28 9JB

The Blue Cross
Shilton Road,
Burford,
Oxon OX18 4PF
01993 822651

The Dogs' Home, Battersea
4 Battersea Park Road,
London SW8 4AA
0171 622 3626

National Canine Defence League
17 Wakely Street,
London EC1V 7LT
0171 837 0006

Royal Society for the Protection of Animals
Causeway,
Horsham,
West Sussex RH12 1HG
01403 264181

The Kennel Club
(for details of breed rescue organisations)
1–5 Clarges Street,
London W1Y 8AB
0171 493 6651

Index

PICTURE CREDITS

Acknowledgements in Source Order
Ardea 56, /John Daniels 17 Bottom, /Jean-Paul Perrero 68 Top
Anne Marie Bazalik 24 Top Left
Chris Barham 6
Gwen Bailey 150 Centre Left
John Daniels 13, 53, 57, 116, 125
David Key 43 Bottom Right, 54 Top
Octopus Publishing Group Ltd. 32 Top, /Rosie Hyde 19, /John Moss 17 Top, /Tim Ridley, 9 right, 10 Centre, 11 Top Left, 11 Top Right, 12, 16, 18, 20 Top Left, 21 Bottom, 22 Top Left, 26, 29 left, 30 Top Left, 30 Top Right, 31 Bottom Right, 34 Main Picture, 35 Main Picture, 36 Top, 37 Bottom, 38 Bottom Left, 39 Centre Right, 40 Top, 42 Bottom Left, 45 Main Picture, 46 Top, 47 Centre Right, 47 Bottom Left, 48 Top, 49 Bottom Left, 51 Top, 55 Bottom Right, 59 Top Left, 60 Top Right, 61 Main Picture, 63, 64 Top, 66 Main Picture, 69 Bottom Right, 71 Top Right, 71 Bottom Left, 73 Main Picture, 74, 76 Main Picture, 78 Centre, 79 Top Left, 80 Top Right, 81 Bottom Right, 82, 84 Top, 85 left, 86, 87, 89, 90 Main Picture, 92 Top Left, 92 Bottom Left, 93 Top Left, 93 Top Right, 93 Centre Centre Right, 93 Centre Right, 93 Bottom Right, 94 Bottom Left, 95 Top Left, 95 Top Centre, 95 Top Right, 95 Centre Right, 95 Bottom Right, 96 Top Left, 96 Centre Left, 96 Centre Right, 97 Top Left, 97 Centre Right, 97 Bottom, 98 Top Left, 98 Top Right, 99 Top, 101 Main Picture, 102 Main Picture, 104 Top, 105 Centre, 106 Top, 107 Bottom, 111 Top, 113 Bottom Right, 114 Main Picture, 117, 119 Main Picture, 122 Top, 126 Main Picture, 129 Bottom Right, 130 Main Picture, 132 Top, 133 Top, 134 left, 137, 138 left, 141, 143 Top, 145 Main Picture, 148 Main Picture, 151 Top, 152 Top Left, 155 Top, 157 Bottom Right
N.H.P.A./T. Kitchin & V. Hurst 67 Bottom, /Norbert Wu 14 Bottom
RSPCA Photolibrary/Angela Hampton 83, /Tim Sambrook 27